Value Education and Society

Dr.K. Dhanalakshmi

Published by

Value Education and Society

Copyright © 2016 by Bonfring

All rights reserved. Authorized reprint of the edition published by Bonfring. No part of this book may be reproduced in any form without the written permission of the publisher.

Limits of Liability/Disclaimer of Warranty: The authors are solely responsible for the contents of the paper in this volume. The publishers or editors do not take any responsibility for the same in any manner. Errors, if any, are purely unintentional and readers are required to communicate such errors to the editors or publishers to avoid discrepancies in future. No warranty may be created or extended by sales or promotional materials. The advice and strategies contained herein may not be suitable for every situation. This work is sold with the understanding that the publisher is not engaged in rendering legal, accounting, or other professional services. If professional assistance is required, the services of a competent professional person should be sought. Further, reader should be aware that internet website listed in this work may have changed or disappeared between when this was written and when it is read.

Bonfring also publishes its books in a variety of electronic formats. Some content that appears in print may not be available in electronic books.

ISBN 978-93-85477-92-8

Author

Dr.K. Dhanalakshmi

Bonfring

309, 2nd Floor, 5th Street Extension,

Gandhipuram, Coimbatore-641 012.

Tamilnadu, India.

E-mail: info@bonfring.org

Website: www.bonfring.org

Phone: 0422-3928700

Preface

From *Vedic age,* value education is continuously followed in India and is guiding all of us. Value education is such a concept which refines human behavior which gives truth, love, beauty, self-control and respect to all and dignity of labor. In *Gurukul education system,* value education started with *Pita Devo Bhava, Mata Devo Bhava, Acharya Devo Bhava and Atithi Devo Bhava.* It means that father, mother, teacher and guest should be respected as God. Values are essential in all fields of education, religion, politics and society. For restructuring of society and nation, value based politics and value based socialization and economic processes are highly essential. All are living in the society where politics are floating with inhuman nature without any ethics and science. Today value education is specially needed for the youth and can play a pivotal role in nation building. It is said that youth is the backbone of nation. Irrespective of age the person, innovative thinking for any developmental process, missionary spirit and mental strength to do anything at any cost may be termed as youth.

It is the right time for the youth for taking part in any developmental activities of the society. With this acquired potentialities, youth can continue nation building activities till to the last day of life. Thinking for welfare of others not only makes one brighter but also brings in benefit to both the persons and the society. Today people have become self-centered and they always think for their own. They are very much attracted to the materialistic world which cannot help in nation building. *Sarvapali Radhakrishnan* stated earlier that the development process in India slowed down because of the division of thinking among the Indians. Collective thinking is very essentials for all developmental processes. It is not possible to hold an elephant by single thread but it is possible to hold the elephant by a bundle of threads. It is because of brotherhood, tolerance and strong social values that the Japanese people are able to achieve highest profile in the world even though they were once destructed by two atom bombs. On this ground, it is to develop student's ability to identify the values embedded, analyse objectively and make reasonable judgments in different issues they may encounter at different developmental stages so that they could take proper action to deal with the challenges in their future life.

Dr.K. Subbammal (Advisor), Vinayaga Mission College of Education, Vinayaga Mission University, Salem and **Late Dr.K. Nirmala,** Department of Education, Periyar University, Salem and my husband **M. Govindaraju** were the inspirations and motivating factor behind in completing this work as a successful.

This book covers the **Syllabus of TNTEU** for the students studying B.Ed., and M.Ed., in the educational institutions.

Dr.K. Dhanalakshmi

<table>
<thead>
<tr><th>Chapter</th><th>Contents</th><th>Page No</th></tr>
</thead>
<tbody>
<tr><td>I</td><td>Introduction</td><td>1</td></tr>
<tr><td></td><td>Values</td><td>1</td></tr>
<tr><td></td><td>Meanings of Values</td><td>2</td></tr>
<tr><td></td><td>Definitions</td><td>3</td></tr>
<tr><td></td><td>Nature of Values</td><td>4</td></tr>
<tr><td></td><td>Concepts of Values</td><td>6</td></tr>
<tr><td></td><td>Characteristics of Values</td><td>6</td></tr>
<tr><td></td><td>Classification of Values</td><td>7</td></tr>
<tr><td></td><td>Instrumental Values</td><td>7</td></tr>
<tr><td></td><td>Personal Values</td><td>8</td></tr>
<tr><td></td><td>Social Values</td><td>8</td></tr>
<tr><td></td><td>Family Values</td><td>9</td></tr>
<tr><td></td><td>Cultural Values</td><td>10</td></tr>
<tr><td></td><td>Democratic Values</td><td>11</td></tr>
<tr><td></td><td>Institutional Values</td><td>11</td></tr>
<tr><td></td><td>Religious Values</td><td>12</td></tr>
<tr><td></td><td>Intrinsic Values</td><td>12</td></tr>
<tr><td></td><td>Component of Values</td><td>13</td></tr>
<tr><td></td><td>Significance of the Values</td><td>13</td></tr>
<tr><td></td><td>NCERT Focused Values</td><td>14</td></tr>
<tr><td></td><td>Indian and Western Views of Values</td><td>16</td></tr>
<tr><td>II</td><td>Value Education towards Personal Development</td><td>17</td></tr>
<tr><td></td><td>Aims of the Value Education</td><td>17</td></tr>
<tr><td></td><td>Objectives of Value Education</td><td>18</td></tr>
<tr><td></td><td>Need for Value Education</td><td>19</td></tr>
<tr><td></td><td>Importance of Value Education</td><td>20</td></tr>
<tr><td></td><td>Values in School Education</td><td>20</td></tr>
<tr><td></td><td>Guidance Programme in Value Education Helps to</td><td>30</td></tr>
<tr><td></td><td>Values in Schools</td><td>32</td></tr>
<tr><td></td><td>Comments of the Various Committees on Value Education</td><td>33</td></tr>
<tr><td></td><td>Status of Value Education in the Present Curriculum</td><td>35</td></tr>
<tr><td></td><td>Role of School in Value Education</td><td>40</td></tr>
</tbody>
</table>

CHAPTER I

Introduction

"Values are conscious or unconscious motivators and justifiers of the actions and Judgment"

T.W.HIPPLE (1969)

Education is the most important invention of mankind. It is more important than the invention of tools machines, space craft, medicine, weapons and even of language to be the product of his education. Man without education would still be living just like an animal. It is education that transformed man from a mere 'two-legged animal' in to human. It helps them to behave like a man and prevents from behaving like an animal.

Values

The term 'values' has been used variously refers to interests, pleasures, likes, preferences, duties, moral obligations, desires, wants, goals, needs, aversions, and attractions, and many other kinds of selective orientations. People are not detached or indifferent to the world and they do not stop with a sheer factual view of their experience. Explicitly or implicitly, they are continually regarding things as good or bad, pleasant, beautiful or ugly, appropriate or inappropriate, true or false, virtues or vices. All values have cognitive, affective and directional aspects. Values serve as criteria selection in action. When most explicit and fully conceptualized, values become criteria for judgment, preference and choice. When implicit and unreflective values 'nevertheless perform 'as if' they constituted grounds for decisions in behavior, Individuals do prefer some things to others, they do select one course of action rather than another out of a range of possibilities and they do judge their own conduct and that of other persons.

Meanings of Values

Values are our personal measure of worth shaped by our beliefs, ideas and principles that are important to us. They shape our priorities and guide us in deciding the right and the wrong. Values reflect our attitudes and those we believe about everything. People value differs and everyone should all learn to tolerate each other values. The power of values arises from the fact that they help us transcend ourselves. Values are to be considered valuable. Placing any ideal of perfection above our own personal convenience and interests expands our personality and opens it to wider and higher influences. The pursuit of higher values is the pursuit of spiritual truth. The expression of higher values is to bring truth down into once life.

Values are our subjective reactions to the world around us. They guide and mould our options and behavior. Values are developed early in life and are very resistant to change. Values develop our direct experiences with people important to us, particularly our parents. Values evolve within us not out of, that people tell us, but as a result of the ways people behave toward us and others. But there cannot be any "partial" values, for example we cannot be half-honest but may be-either honest or not honest. A value is a belief, a mission, or a philosophy that is meaningful. Whether people are consciously aware of them or not, every individual has a core set of personal values. Values can range from the commonplace, such as the belief in hard work and punctuality, to the more psychological, such as self-reliance, concern for others, and harmony of purpose.

Definitions

Values are perceived differently by different philosophers as follows, that help us to understand the meaning of values. Value is an element of shared symbolic system that serves as a criterion or standard for selection among the alternatives of orientation, intrinsically open to a situation.

T.Patter Parson (1960)

Values are the ideals, beliefs or norms that a society or the large majority of a society's members holds.

Kane (1962)

Values are the integral part of personal philosophy of life, we generally mean the system of values by the way people live. The philosophy of life includes our aims, ideals and manner of thinking and the principles in guiding our behavior and conducts our crisis.

I.J.Lehner & N.J.Kube (1967)

Values are the principles and fundamental convictions that act as general guides to behavior, the standards for particular actions that are to be judged as good or desirable.

Halstead, Taylor and Taylor (2000)

Values are the priorities of individuals and society, attached to certain beliefs, experiences, and objects in deciding the ways shall live and that they shall treasure.

Hill (2004)

"The value means primarily to prize, to esteem, to appraise and estimate. It means the act of cherishing something holding it dear and also the act of passing judgment upon the nature and amount as values of compared with something else"

John Dewey (1939)

It has been pointed out that man acts go satisfy their needs, anything that satisfies a human need becomes there by value. Our conduct is motivated by our value is another way of saying that individuals act to satisfy our needs.

Henderson (2011)

"A value is that is desired or sought. Values may be operationally, conceived as those guiding principles of life that are conductive to one's physical and mental health as well as to social welfare and adjustment and in tune with one's culture"

N.T.Ram (2011)

"Value is an element of shared symbolic system that serves as a criterion or standard for selection among the alternatives of orientation, intrinsically open to a situation"

T. Pater Parson (1960)

"Values are emotional judgments generated by feelings not cognition. They are emotional, not intellectual judgments"

R.Borzoi (2011)

Nature of Values

- Values are standards or guidelines for an individual's life
- Values are the guidelines for a nation that guide its policies
- Values are learned and acquired in many ways
- values steer or life's journey
- Values are not static and they change with time
- Values are influenced by emotions
- Anything that has utility is a value

- Values are hierarchical in nature
- Values are helpful for survival
- Values frequently represent alternative
- The values are based on the past experiences, learned behavior, traditions or logic of the community.
- The values have three components:
- Cognitive,
- Emotional, and
- Behavioral.

Theory based Nature of Values

There are four views about understanding the nature of values. They are (i) The interest Theory (ii) The Existence Theory (iii) The Experimental Theory and (iv) The Part Whole Theory.

i. **Interest Theory:** It is subjective. It tells whether a person desires something that has a value for himself. Values depend upon the person's interest. It is a Realistic Theory.

ii. **Existence Theory:** It holds that values exist in their own right, irrespective of the values or his interests. They exist independently in their own right. It is an idealistic Theory.

iii. **Experimental Theory:** It holds only that value that yields a greater sense of happiness in the present and promises still more of it in future. They are no permanent values. This is a Pragmatic Theory.

iv. **Part-Whole Theory:** It holds to realize and enjoy value, one must effectively relate parts to the whole.

Concepts of Values

To understand and study values seriously, one should be aware of the following concepts

- **Value Diversity** : diversity of values
- **Value Change** : Changes taking place in values
- **Value Neutrality**: Observing neutrality or objectivity in matters of value.
- **Value Judgment** : Judging or assessing values
- **Value Interpretation** : Analysis and interpretation of values
- **Value Distortion**: **Values** presented as distortion, unfairly criticized or mocked at.
- **Value Conflicts or Value Tensions:** Conflicts or tensions in two or more sets of values or in two or more groups of people having different values.

Characteristics of Values

The following are the characteristics of values

- The values of a community, society or culture are considered to be proper or worthwhile in that society or culture. The Indian values are held high by the people of India.
- They are accepted, approved or shared by most or many of the people of the given community or cultural group.
- They are the recognized modes or patterns of beliefs, thinking and behaviour.
- People are emotionally attached to their values. They become their cultural habits of thinking and behaviour.
- The values of a society or cultural group exert their pressure on its members, motivate and incline or compel its members to act according them.

- Values are the essential and permanent component of group interaction in a society, and they have the same place in social sciences as the place natural laws have in physical sciences
- Although the values of a society or group are usually permanent or long lasting, yet in a changing society or changed physical or socio-cultural environment they may also change, weaken or even get extinct.
- In the strong flow of values, social institution may get changed, weakened or even disappear.
- Values are expressed while people perform their various social roles, formal roles as well informal roles in their society.
- Values are a means of unity, cohesion or solidarity.

Classification of Values

Values as principles and fundamental convictions are abstractions until they are applied in the contexts of daily life. Values are made real or realized when its meaning is expressed through choices made and behaviors acted out. There are a number of value domains that derive from the contexts, individuals live their lives and conduct their relationships. Most commonly talked about values turn out to be talk about matters of morality. There are different kinds of values that people acquire and support to different degrees and the value profile of one person differs from the value profile of another person. Hence, Values have been classified in various ways.

Instrumental Values

Instrumental values are values that are instrumental in getting desired ends. They are useful only in that they are acceptable ways of behaving. These are values that can be used to get something else. In other words the value is an instrument that allows us to get some other things in socially accepted ways

Instrumental values can be viewed as having 'evolved'. The best values that create successful societies.

Examples of instrumental values include Personal Values, Social Values, Family Values, Cultural Values, Democratic Values, and institutional Values

Personal Values

"That civilization perishes in that the individual

Thwarts the revelation of the universal"

Rabindranath Tagore

Personal values are cherished and practiced by an individual within oneself without any explicit interaction with any other person. Examples are cleanliness, integrity, punctuality, self-discipline, honesty, simple living, courage, self- confidence sincerity, ambition, independence, hard work, mature self, contentment etc.,

Personal values are deeply held a belief that guides the behaviors and decisions. It resides deeply within the subconscious and is tightly integrated into the fabric of everyday living. It helps us to make decisions and choose behaviors, friends, employment, and entertainment.

Social Values

"Humanity could only have survived and flourished if it held

social and personal values that transcended the urges of the

individual, embodying selfish desires and these stem from the

sense of a transcendent good"

Arthur Peacocke

Social Values are cherished and practiced because of our association with others. Social values necessarily bring in interaction of two or more persons. It is related to neighbors, community, society, nation, and the world. World becomes a better place to live in because of social values. Examples of social values are cooperativeness, tolerance, service to others, dignity of labour, orderliness, social responsibility, sociability, helpfulness, gratitude, sympathy, righteous conduct, adjusted, environment preservation,sense of belongingness, hospitality, magnanimity, sportsmanship, sharing, brotherhood etc.,

Belief in the brotherhood of humankind, adaptability and tolerance the unifying factors promoting peace and harmony between people are indispensable for national integration and world peace. Living in a pluralistic, multilingual society, representing divergent religious beliefs, cultures and lifestyles, necessitates the practice of these social values. Particularly exercise of tolerance enables us to accept differences in a spirit of understanding and friendliness.

Family Values

"In every conceivable manner, the family is link to

Our past, bridge to our future"

Alex Haley

Family traditions are usually defined as 'a combination of social ideals, personal attitudes, ideas, and environment derived from our parents or relatives, while family values usually refer to ways many of us frame our personal life in our relationship with our family members to maintain harmony.' Examples are compassion, reverence and respect for elders, sound health, love, tolerance, hygienic living, obedience, happiness, cheerful commitment, empathy, mutual respect, mutuality, patience etc.

The values of a family will depend on the dynamics of the family it will also depend on education, culture, and the society the family lives in. Religious preference is likely to be determined under our family value. This will be different for each family as well as for each generation. It is not uncommon for family values to change as society changes.

As values are integrated with culture, religion as well as socially determined attitudes, behaviour and customs, an evaluative and critically questioning methodology is required for the promotion of family values. In course of social change people adopt new ways of living, old customs and practices fail to make meaning to younger generations. Hence, the need for introducing meaningful values becomes a necessity.

Cultural Values

"If you see in any given situation only what

Everybody else can see, you can be said to be so much

A representative of your culture that you are a victim of it"

S.I. Hayakawa

Cultural Values are commonly held standards of the acceptable or unacceptable, important or unimportant, right or wrong, workable or unworkable in a community or society. Examples are social order, tolerance, liberty, gentleness, non-violence, love etc. A cultural value may serve as a function in a particular situation and circumstance, but in no way can it be seen as the only or the best way of doing things. A spoon can serve the function of lifting food but so can a fork, a knife, a spatula or bare fingers. Creative development of ideas often emerges out of an interaction of different cultural values and an understanding and respect for differences. Cultural values are reflected in language, ethics, social hierarchy, aesthetics, education, law, economics, philosophy and social institutions of every kind.

Democratic Values

"If we value independence, we are disturbed the

Growing conformity of knowledge, of values, of

Attitudes, that our present system induces, then we

May wish to set up conditions of learning that

Make for uniqueness, far self-direction, and far self -

Initiated learning"

Carl Rogers

Democratic Values are the fundamental beliefs and constitutional principles of our society. Examples of democratic values are common good, justice, liberty, popular sovereignty, equality, diversity and pursuit of happiness, truth, patriotism, rule of law, community service, dutifulness, humanism, justice, non-violence, secularism, universal love, citizenship, discipline, national integration, peace, freedom, and equality.

Non-violence or Ahimsa is the virtue of never causing pain to any living being by thought, word or deed. The cardinal foundations of non-violence are fearlessness, chastity, non-attachment and truth. Truth, patriotism, rule of law, humanism, and justice should be activated at different levels to oneself, person to person, person to group, group to group as democratic values for the welfare of the nation.

Institutional Values

Institutional values are beliefs that endure over time about conduct or activities. Dominant institutional values exhibit four characteristics such as extensiveness throughout the system, durability over a considerable period of time, intensity shown by choices and verbal affirmation, and prestige of those espouse the values.

Examples: leadership, initiative, regularity, curiosity, spirit of enquiry, team spirit, loyalty to duty, resourcefulness, genuineness, intellect, politeness, productiveness, flexibility, ethics, creativity, accountability etc.

Religious Values

Religious values are nothing but virtues- insisted by religions of the world that are always focused on peace and goodness. The Examples are faith in God, respect for all religions, purity, self-reliance, devotion, forgiveness, kindness, sacrifice, truth, non-violence, humility etc. A person having a bundle of religious values will also exhibit humility in their way in approaching things. Humility is defined as a quality by that a person considering his own defects has a bumble opinion of himself and willingly submits himself to God and to others for God's sake.

Intrinsic Values

An intrinsic value is used to refer to the value an object has solely by virtue of its 'intrinsic properties'. Something has intrinsic worth simply because of that it is and not necessarily will lead to or because of its acceptance. Some possible examples of intrinsic values would include goodness, beauty, artistic expression, and happiness, truth and bliss. Peace is internal and it is the greatest power because when people lose their peace they get emotional and start doing all kinds of things that don't make any sense. One should learn to maintain peace in our relationships with God, with themselves and with fellowmen.

It is easy to lose our peace when someone hurts us; the only way to get along with people is to be generous with forgiveness. Peace is purposeful when maintained leads to highest level of productivity in mental and physical health. Unless peace Works as intrinsic factor, people can' maintain good health.

Component of Values

A value has three pronged structure that covers all the possible aspects of human personality.

Cognitive Aspect – Thought

A value is an idea abstract in nature. More is the idea clear, strong will be the value. Therefore it is to be assumed that a value is related to mental activity and cognitive development about an idea, through or an object.

Affective Aspect – Emotional / Feeling

A value possess a strong emotional bound with idea, thought or material object. Happy association is the secret of a value. Feeling, sentiment and attitudes are involved in one's value structure. In fact, values are the cherished goals, preferences or desired thing. Involvement of emotion and feeling is the secret for one's, pleasure giving in the long run.

Cognitive / Psychomotor Aspect – Action/behaviour

A value results into an action of behavior. This aspect is the final stage or culmination of a value. The first two aspects i.e. cognitive (idea) and effective (emotion/feeling) pave the way for action. Therefore 'action' is the acidic test of one's value in life.

Significance of the Values

Education plays a very great role in the society. Among that value education is very important in order to make a man to live a meaningful life. A life without proper value will become chaotic and disastrous. It will be a boat without rudder. To guide our life in the right path and to embellish our behavior with good qualities we need value education.

Value education is important to develop the behavioral changes in human being. It helps to enhance the respect, honesty, simplicity, self-confidence among every human create with value education we can shape the everyone. Transmission of human values is to be made feasible by the pivotal role played by the Teacher in the arena. Teacher is the right person to develop awareness and sensitivity of duties and values amongst the children. An efficient teacher aims at enlightening the minds and values amongst the children. An efficient teacher aims at enlightening the minds and illumining the hearts of individual. Teachers are the strong pillar of nation. It is in the hands of teachers to mould the personality of the students by inculcation of values.

The role of a teacher was limited to being a source of information. But today this place is shared by books, coaching classes, multimedia technology etc. So the role of a teacher is marginalized. Role of a teacher has increased manifold. A teacher can maintain values and nurture them. A teacher has an immense potential of bringing about a see change in the society by demonstrating essential values of head and heart. Teacher can impart values in students by giving them instructions through discussion, experimentation and lectures. The role of teachers is quite significant in the development of social values. Teachers are the real nation builders. It is the teaching community that moulds the future society. The development of any country depends upon it educational system. Any type of development is possible trough teachers.

NCERT Focused Values

NCERT has worked out 82 values. These values are related to all categories of human experience at three planes like body, mind and spirit.

Body

- Simple living
- Duty

- Cleanliness

Mind

- Fellow feeling
- Sympathy
- Honesty
- Concern for other
- Socialism and respect for all religious
- Humanism
- Good Manner
- Self-discipline
- Self Confidence
- Self-control
- Self-respect

Spirit

- Devotion
- Sense of social responsibility
- Good manners
- Truthfulness
- Patriotism
- Gentle manliness
- Quest for knowledge
- Compassion
- Spirit of enquiry
- Gratitude
- Loyalty of duty
- Kindness to animal
- Reverence for old age

- Universal love

- Peace

- National consciousness

- Friendship

- Endurance

- Common good

Indian and Western Views of Values

Indian View of Values

It derives from a socio–philosophic tradition with roots deep in the past. Unlike the west, philosophy in India could not free itself completely from the hold of religion. Philosophy to the ancient Indians was not just a means of satisfying intellectual doubt (samsaya) but more, a practical endeavor then showed one the right way to attain spiritual liberation (mocha), the sum mum bonus of life (purusharthas), economic value wellbeing (artha), physical wellbeing (kama), righteous action (dharma) and spiritual freedom (moksha) , the secular values of artha and kama rank inferior in status in the Indian hierarchy of values, to the spiritual values of dharma and moksha. Even among the letter, moksha is far higher than dharma. In fact, it is the highest end of human life, it being freedom from the very notion of right and wrong and the good and bad.

Western Concept of Values

In the west, the traditional position claiming the inseparability of religion and values has almost been replaced by the view that knowledge in values is autonomous in the sense that it does not necessarily depend on religion, that an act is essentially a rational act and concept of person with values as a rationally autonomous individual. It is not doing good or acting right but acting so far the right reasons that constitutes the essence of morality.

CHAPTER II

VALUE EDUCATION TOWARDS PERSONAL DEVELOPMENT

Aims of the Value Education

As an organized social institution has been considered a major vehicle for nurturance of values. Conceptually, the objectives of education encompass education for values. At the practical level, however, 'value education is referred to as a deliberately planned education aimed at the development of proper attitudes, values, emotions ultimately teach intellectual, spiritual, civic, and moral aspects of life. This will ensure well-rounded and balanced individuals. Educators should strive to develop a quality education system that satisfies the needs of the individual and society. Educators should focus on full energy and endless efforts to give all children, regardless of their background, and an equal opportunity to receive the best education. Thus value 'education must aim at

- Achieving humanistic attitude in the students mind.
- Helping the students to have a simple and fairly comprehensive knowledge about the concept and the significance of values in life.
- Instigating students to select their own–positive personal, social, moral and spiritual values and be aware of ways for developing and deepening them as global citizens.
- Guiding life in the right path 'and to embellish behaviour with good qualities.
- Developing a sense of pride about our rich heritage and ancient wisdom by showing them how these principles and truths are in perfect accord with modern science.
- Providing students with a foundation for ethical reasoning that includes the core values of integrity, objectivity and independence.

- Providing guidance to the students concerning the ethical rules and regularities of the society and professional accounting.

- To understand the national goals of socialism, secularism, social justice and democracy and to contribute to their consciousness.

- Helping teachers to conduct the class in a professional and ethical manner that models behavior that students may be expected to display as a professional accountant.

Objectives of Value Education

- To inculcate in the students respect for their culture and gratitude to their parents, teachers, nation and all those who strive for their welfare.

- To enable students to be the balanced personality and to make them refined with perfection.

- To develop individuality of the child through really practical, useful and purposive contents and methodology of value education.

- To make students understand our heritage, national goals and universal perceptions through value education curriculum, so as to become a more sensitive and responsible citizen.

- To develop a critical consciousness to analyze human development down the ages.

- To help students lay a strong foundation for the development of different values.

- To enable students to clarify conflicts based on education.

- To provide a realistic and broad-based understanding of human values and to educate/train students to become responsible citizens in their personal and social lives.

- To enable students to understand, appreciate, uphold, protect and promote the sovereignty, unity and integrity of India and the national goals of egalitarianism, socialism secularism and democracy besides imbibing values enshrined in the Indian Constitution.

- To protect, preserve and conserve the natural and cultural environment and to make judicious use of natural resources.
- To enable students to distinguish between good and bad, right and wrong and acquire intellectual wisdom and disposition to do ethically correct and good.

Need for Value Education

- The modern materialistic world raises our standard of living but declines our standards of life, i.e., The Value of life on account of population explosion, knowledge explosion (science and technology) and material explosion, man has started moving towards the wrong path by considering material comforts of the world as the real happiness.
- In fact from the nineties the erosion of human values at all levels and everywhere in the present society, leading to the spread of greed, self-aggrandizement gross injustice, abuse of human rights, pervasion of power, callousness, insensitivity, depravity, of taste and behavior, pettiness, water and plunder, deceit, dishonestly, thefts, bribery, smuggling, corruption, exploitation, craftiness and man's wallowing in the low and dark dimensions of his consciousness
- The growing influence of the negative aspects of the western culture on the younger generation is standard on the crossroads. It is very necessary to dispel this pollution spreading in the society, so that we can preserve and maintain the advanced position of our country.

Importance of Value Education

The present educational system, with all its complexities has proved to be deficient in so far as it neglects or does not give the deserving importance to values in human life. Thus human sufferings and sorrows are forever on the increase in spite of the phenomenal explosion of knowledge value have become the neglected lot in the current educational system and consequently the maximum "education changes man" ceases to be meaningful or has almost lost its value is crime "education without vision is waste, education without mission is life burden".

Education in our life enables us to become comfortable and to look after our family well. But so far the social progress is concerned value, based education is an unavoidable necessity. If a nation is to be strong the character of the people of that nation needs to be elevated.

Values in School Education

Ancient Culture

India has and had a rich cultural heritage of over five thousand years. Cumulative and dynamic dimensions of intellectual, moral and spiritual culture of our ancient people have made it very rich. It comprises eternal truths and spiritual experiences of many great seers. It consists of prayers, methods and techniques of moral and spiritual training, moral discussions, revealed knowledge of innumerable sages, teachings of universal teachers, very good sayings, virtues possessed by noteworthy kings and great leaders, stories about gods and goddesses, biographies of the elite, values practiced by noble men, intellectual dialogues between teachers and students, views of laity about the life, rituals, customs and habits of our ancestors.

Present Scenario

The present scene in our country is discouraging. Today our country is at cross-roads. At no time in the past, India had faced as many problems as one can see today. Thousands of ills are multiplied and intensified. Almost all our ancient moral and spiritual portals are eclipsed by ignorance, present values are covered by thick layers of corruption, virtues have completely vanished, vices occupied the place of virtues, peace has given room to chaos and confusion, guile has penetrated into all walks of life, the guiltless people are punished while the guilty are going free, good habits are replaced by bad, cultured families have become uncultured, almost everybody desires ill-gotten wealth, egotism has reached its peak, new and new controversial issues and scandals are coming up day after day, corruption has spread its dreadful tentacles everywhere, political power has become poisoned, terrorists are threatening the country, and illegal activities are undertaken by the so-called law-abiding leaders. Therefore the entire life is pervaded by social evils and everyone is in confusion.

There are a number of obstacles that act as decelerators in the implementation of value education in our schools. Mis-interpretation of our ancient values and traditions by many leaders and politicians and malpractices of our people are the major blocks in this process. As long as individuals are unable to realize the significance of values in our life till then the implementation of value programme would be definitely an up-hill task.

Past verses Present Education

During Pre-Vedic period (about 3000 BC to 1600 BC), Vedic period (about 1600 BC to 550 BC) and post-Vedic period (about 500 BC to 200 AD), no regular schools and universities were present in our country. Therefore no formal education was provided to the masses. Usually the prime sources of knowledge were the seers or the scholarly people in those days and they were imparting the sacred knowledge with utmost care to a few selected students. These elite teachers or acharyas (sources of knowledge) were either living in forests or at the outskirts of habitations. The seekers of knowledge (students) were always living with their teachers till the completion of their studies. The teachers were imparting sacred knowledge to their disciples without prejudice. Even students 'had full faith in their teachers and devoted to their studies and duties. Shisyas (Students) were undergoing very strict and disciplined training under the able guidance of learned teachers. Every one of them was striving to obtain spiritual experiences through different austerities. Hence all of them were enjoying eternal bliss at the end of their education. As a result, values were considered as inseparable parts of human activities. The nature of these activities was determined by the type of education provided to them. Education was equated with the four-fold values viz., dharma, artha, kama and moksha.

As time passed by, the house of a preceptor was converted into a seat of learning. This type of seat of learning was termed as 'gurukula'. Once the student was accepted by a teacher, he was treated as a member of the gurukula. The student was totally devoted to his guru and gurukula. He rendered his services to the guni and his wife whole- heartedly and sincerely. Individual attention to the needs of the learner was totally assured at all costs, once the grace of the guru was obtained. The mode of instruction was 'word-of-mouth'.

A similar type of education was continued with minor changes even during the intellectual period (about 200 AD to 1250 AD). Institutes such as Nalanda and Takshashila were opened and became seats of higher learning. Here dwarapalakas (gatekeepers) themselves conducted preliminary interviews for the seekers of knowledge. Only those that were successful were allowed to enter the institute. Three steps to learning sravana (careful listening of the utterings of teacher), manana (reflection or the constant contemplation of what was heard) and nidhidhyasana (concentrated contemplation of what was reflected) were very common. Tapa (austerity was the base for these three steps. Individualized instruction was predominant in the education system. Each individual was allowed to learn according to his capabilities. Dialogues (questions, further questions and cross-questions), explanations, enquiries and practical methods formed a part of the main stream of education.

Even a few itinerant (wandering) teachers were also responsible for imparting informal education. Debating circles/ parishads / conferences courts were usually the main centres of enrichment of knowledge. The aim of education was to produce men of character. Understanding of life and techniques in the art of living were the important ingredients of education. Influence of foreign cultures (about 1200 AD to 1750 AD) led to the starting of Pathashalas and Madrassas in our country. Pandits struggled hard to retain the ancient culture and values in Pathashalas. Foreign Moulvis tried to impart foreign culture in this land. As a result, cultures were diffused and values got mixed. But this diffusion and mixture were not very harmful to society.

During the colonial period (about 1750) AD until independence), the British system of education was imposed by the rulers on us. A number of schools were opened along the lines of the British system of education to produce a large number of clerks, to get the work of masters in this country. The language of the rulers became the language of instruction. Undue weightage was given to stereotype examinations. Mere getting degrees and obtaining certificates became the primary objective of the student-community. Mass education led to the deterioration in the quality of education. Indian values were never conceived as the prime requisite for good citizenship by Britishers.

After independence, the Sovereign Democratic Republic of India launched a programme of democratisation and universalisation of education. Many efforts were made at the government and grass-root levels, to put into practice the basic principles of democracy and the cultural values in the system of school education. But deep rooted corruption in the minds of common man and selfish politicians' attitude caused obstacles to the process of democratisation of education. As a result, commercialisation of education encompassed the whole gamut of present day educational machinery. Even the lop-sided industrialisation of education has its bad influence on education system. Hence the divine learning centres became commercial centres and dedicated teachers at once became wage-earners. Seekers of knowledge became raw materials in the education market. Certified candidates are treated as ready made goods. Money and political power are the major qualifications for the certified candidates to get jobs rather than intellectual capacity and merit. Hence influential candidates occupy white-collared jobs in the employment market. Realisation of this fact by parents forced them to pay heavy amounts of money as bribe and donations either for getting seats in prestigious schools and colleges or to get jobs. Since managers took the role of business transactors, newly employed persons became the promoters of corruption.

In short, past and present system of education projects diametrically opposite facts and figures. The entire system of education was based on good virtues and values of the past. Today, it is full of voices and evil practices. In the past, character building and nation building education was the prime objects of curriculum. Curriculum is content centered at present. Mastery of the subject matter and self-learning were objectives of past education. Certification and getting jobs are objectives of present education. Self-realisation was the ultimate aim of education in olden days.

Yearning for power and getting money by any means seem to be ultimate aim of today's education. Education in the past was training of individuals to face any kind of challenge in their life. They were independent in thinking and taking decisions. But today, our education is so ineffective in developing courage and confidence in individuals. They are not capable of standing on their own feet. They are not prepared to face the problems of life. Everyone becomes dependent on others. Moral values flowed in the blood of our fore-fathers. But today, vices seem to be in the blood of our people. The earlier guru was the embodiment of all virtues and he was the role model to his disciples. Now, most of the teachers are not fit for their jobs. They are not committed to their profession and hence students have no role model to follow. In the past, values were interwoven in the system of education and there was no need to talk about value education. No one was required to teach value education separately. But today, since everyone has forgotten the significance of values, there is a dire need for value education for everybody.

Erosion of Values

Decline of values began with the invasions of foreigners to this country. Besides this, internal conflicts and evil practices rose to the maximum during the company rule. Recent development in different disciplines of knowledge such as Physics, Chemistry, Biology, Mathematics, Geology, Astronomy, Oceanology, Meteorology, Technology, Engineering, Medicine, etc., without the parallel development in value systems, sudden explosion of population in this century, particularly in our country, rapid increase of environmental pollution, increase in illiteracy rate, scarcity of essential food grains, dearth of commodities, soaring prices, continuous depletion of natural resources, increase in problems of employment, imbalance in the ecosystem, decrease in quality of life, low standard of living when compared to other countries, increase of multi-fold problems in education, low per capita income, increase of illegal encroachment of forest areas and agricultural lands and deforestation, lack of morality in teachers, administrators, lawyers, doctors, politicians, judges, business people, etc., in their professions, increasing egotism, jealousy, enmity, hatred and greediness in everybody, corruption, adulteration, cheating, looting, robbery, terrorist or militant activities and disputes are increasing in an alarming rate, political hypocrisies and criminalization in all the fields are further intensifying the rate of decay of values in our country. Bulimia is another major cause for erosion of values. Poverty motivates people to involve in anti-social activities. Even cultured people are forgetting their own rich past culture and blindly imitating the Western culture. Hence the steep fall of values are observed during the century.

Distortion of values is partially due to imbalance between ancient values and explosion of knowledge in war field technology. Atomic weapons, bio-weapons, explosives, missiles etc., are threatening the whole man-kind. Developed countries possess all types of dreadful modern weapons and trying to boss over developing and underdeveloped countries. Today, the entire mankind is living in the shade of fearful atmosphere. Man's very existence is at stake and hence he is indulging himself in all wicked activities.

The role of home, school and society cannot be neglected in the degradation of values. Definitely the living styles of parents leave deep impressions in the minds of children. Usually every child imitates virtues and voices of parents. Petty quarrels at home between husband and wife, parents and children, elders and youngsters, frequent use of vulgar language in socio-economic backward families, bad habits of elders and poverty at home are responsible for disimprovement of value system in our country. Prostitution, illegal marriage, broken home structure, divorce etc., are the main factors in the decline of values. Lack of mutual concern between each other at home, dis-affection and lack of security in families are other factors responsible for the erosion of values. Fall in values is mainly due to non-conducive environment present in our schools. School education will definitely play a vital role in modeling and nurturing the future life of an individual. An upsurge in enrolment rate of students in educational institutions, lack of essential facilities and resources in schools, imbalance between teacher-student ratio, increase of mechanical book-learning or cook-book system of education, faulty evaluation schemes followed by schools and authorities, faulty policies of the government, worst type of political influences in schools, wrong attitude of teachers toward their profession and teaching, illegal and immoral home tuitions from kindergarten level to higher education, no job-security for teachers and also very low salary for teachers in many management schools, highly ambitious parents with regard to performance, progress and future job opportunities 'of their children, commercialization of education, aimless student communities, students disinterest in studies, loaded curriculum without values, agitations, protests, bundhs, boycotts, cheating and malpractices in examinations, aggressive behaviour of students, dis-respect to teachers and elders, increasing indiscipline in schools, ragging in hostels, increasing cynicism, smoking, drinking, drug-addiction, gambling, etc., are the source factors in decay of values in schools.

Modern society has no set moral standards. Sense of responsibility and belongingness to a group are completely vanished. Mutual respect and consideration for others are disappearing. Social gatherings and group activities are organized without giving due weightage to values. Communities are disunited. Community clashes are very common in these days. Blind westernization failed to inculcate virtues in people but still it is continued. Evil activities are increasing day by day. Cynicism has spoiled everybody. It is rightly observed by the members of National Education Policy (NEP, 1986) the growing concern over the erosion of essential values and an increasing cynicism in society has brought to focus the need for readjustments in the curriculum in order to make education a forceful tool for the cultivation of social and moral values. This observation indicates that the present day education has failed to cultivate necessary and sufficient social and moral values in the members of society. Hence values get no better fast in our society.

Recent Challenges

Many countries disappeared in the past due to the deathblow of value system. Historical events are sign-posts in this regard. Unpleasant events in history repeat itself when precautions are not taken. Therefore when the country forgets this fact, it will go to the bad and then it is put in peril. At present, India is at stake since eternal values are masked by modern socio political corrupt systems and sheaths of ignorance are covered the rich ancient values. It is not a wonder that if decay of values continues further, then within a few centuries India may perish. Therefore it is the responsibility of everybody to preserve and put in practice the rich ancient values.

Human life is meaningful and worth considered only when values are part and parcel of day to day activities, Right education inculcates right values in individuals right education gives direction to individual's life. Right education alone is the perfect education. Right education is capable of converting job-centered education into work-centered education. Therefore right education should be provided to every citizen of the country at right time. Shouldering responsibility and solving problem demands hard work, co-ordination, co-operation, whole hearted participation, attitudinal change and sacrifice from everybody.

The pursuit of eternal happiness must be one of the chiefs aims of education and not mere possessing and developing material comforts in this life. The flexible, broad and humane curriculum must provide opportunities to inculcate values in students by all means. The life of the school must be the fountain-head of values. The school should provide ennobling and elevating experience to students. School must have facilities to inculcate values in students and should create the useful life-environment for their progress. Creation of life-environment in school requires change in its atmosphere.

There is no dearth of value resources in our country. We have rich traditions, customs, habits, rituals, social functions, festivals, etc. Our country is a multilingual and multi-cultural glorious land. It is the abode of thirty three crores of Gods and Goddesses. It is the dwelling place of many sages, noblemen and poets. "As we sow so we reap" cannot be forgotten. Existing problems of today definitely yield corresponding fruits either today itself or in future. Present day problems are due to unnatural deeds. Therefore the results are also of this nature. It is very apt to quote Shakespear's words here 'Unnatural deeds give unnatural fruits'. Put to an end to the unnatural deeds is a great challenge to us.

Television serials, cinemas, video and audio recordings, modellings, advertisements, magazines, modern novels, etc., have adverse effect on students behaviour and character development. The astonishing fact in this regard is the grand encouragement by the public. The attitude of the public has to be changed once for all. It is not an easy task. Value education becomes meaningless without solving this serious problem. Well known dictum is "practice is better than precept". Creation of role models in this modern technical world is really a challenging task. Swami Vivekananda says that education by that character is formed strength of mind is increased, the intellect is expanded and by that one can stand on one's own feet. But education at present is completely divorced from Swami Vivekananda concept of education. This is due to lack of individual guidance and group guidance programmes in value education. Hence there is a dire need for individual guidance and group guidance for teachers, parents, administrators and policy makers with regard to inculcation of values in students.

Guidance Programme in Value Education Helps to

- Develop self-confidence, courage and strength in individuals and in group to face new challenges in education.
- Eradicate the racial discrimination on the basis of color, caste and creed.
- Foresee present and future problems in the field of education.
- Develop the all-round human personality.
- Utilize artificial and natural resources to the maximum extent for the welfare of society.
- Improve the standard of life.
- Improve the quality of life.
- Develop self-discipline in every body.
- Realize responsibilities of everybody(i.e., students, teachers, administrators and policy makers) in practicing and promotion of values.
- Appreciate rich ancient culture.
- Enrich past culture.
- Transmit undistorted ancient culture to present and coming generations.
- Prevent and remove social evils such as drug addiction, smoking, drinking, gambling, etc.
- Realize adverse effects of misutilisation of mass media.
- Realize the significance of developing morality and spirituality in every body.

- Develop the attitude and importance of involvement in socially useful activities.

- Realize the importance of moral commitment in the accepted assignment.

- Think morally, solve problems independently and take moral decisions.

- Inculcate virtues such as honesty, truthfulness, sincerity etc.

- Keep the inner-guide (consciousness) in the waking state.

- Develop inner strength to realize the reality of life.

- Reverse the divergent energy (i.e., divergent into convergent).

- Focus energy towards self (act like a convergent lens).

- Create a favorable, atmosphere conducive for virtue development in students.

- Develop right opinions and right attitudes toward value.

- Develop good citizenship qualities in students.

- Develop the concept of unity, integration and international brotherhood in students.

- Practice silence, prayer and meditation for self-elevation in life.

- Practice and appreciate devotional songs.

- Develop strong and noble character.

- Develop respect for chosen profession.

- Develop value oriented curriculum.

- Prepare value oriented textbooks.

- Use appropriate method of value education in schools.

- Organize value oriented training programme for teachers, parents and administrators.

- Organize value oriented curricular and co-curricular programmes in schools.

- Utilize timely service from voluntary organizations such as redcross, traffic police, NCC, NSS, scouts and guides, etc.
- Appreciate the significance of observation of festivals, days of importance of national leaders, scientists, philosophers, etc., in promotion of values.
- Organize counselling services in schools for value promotion, and
- Develop national ideas in everybody.

Values in Schools

Values Education Occurs in Schools in Five Main Ways

The decisions of Boards of Trustees (BOT), principals and the policies agreed on constitute powerful moral lessons. When schools chose bulk funding because "we could not turn the money down" they were announcing their moral stance. When school principals promote their school on the basis of exam results, they are being dishonest, as professionals they must have read the literature that shows that almost all the variance between schools on public exams is explained by the kind of students go there, a powerful lesson about honesty. When schools poach students of talented and decline to enroll their share of children with special needs they are shouting their values from the school tops. When they accept business sponsorship they pronounce that money is more important than the impartiality as necessary for good education. A school interested in values should start at the top.

The power relations in schools and the way these are handled constitute daily lessons in values. They show the ways of the principal views their staff, teachers view each other, teachers view students, and the school views parents. Pious exhortations on kindness and fairness will be perceived by students (and rightly) as further examples of adult hypocrisy unless the relationships are benign, professional and consultative.

The rules of the school are themselves models of what the school values. Rational rules necessary for the smooth running of the school have to be distinguished from those that violate the student's civil rights and those that merely reflect the narrow mindedness of the community. Rules that affect students every day are teaching powerful lessons about morality.

There are some moral values that must be accepted and unchallenged in the school for they safeguard persons as moral agents. Thus, no school can tolerate racism, sexism, hate speech, violent behaviour, harassment, bullying or theft. Although some of these may be debated at the highest level of philosophical argument they cannot be tolerated in practice in the school since each child has to be seen as a person with equal rights and the school as a moral community that acknowledges these rights.

The role of the school is to promote critical reflection on morality. Programmes of values education, linked to classroom subjects or assemblies, should not be forms of indoctrination into one set of values since this is a democratic and pluralistic society.

Comments of the Various Committees on Value Education

Some advocate the view that values have to be promoted through curriculum. In some universities and colleges, for some years, syllabus was prepared for the teaching of values and according to that, moral instruction classes were conducted. Promotion of the study of humanities and social sciences like literature, history and culture and making all students study some prominent pieces of the humanities and social sciences, it is argued, will provide liberal education at the higher level resulting in the dissemination of noble values. But in this computer era, students are not evincing any interest in humanities and social sciences. Making the study of something related to values compulsory, may not have the desired effect.

- The **Radhakrishnan Commission** (1948) gave importance to the inculcation of ethical values among students not only in colleges but also in universities. As per the recommendations of that Commission, provision W28'made for moral instruction in colleges and universities. The Kothari Commission that was appointed in 1965 and declared that 'knowledge with a lack of essential values may be dangerous'.

- Apart from the reports of the education commissions, the recent declaration of the UNESCO on higher Education has also clearly proclaimed the need for promotion of values through Higher Education. The International Conference on Higher Education held in 1998 and attended by about 18D countries declared that importance should be given to the dissemination of universally accepted values like freedom, justice and equality. The UNESCO declaration on Higher Education has also focused 'attention on involving students in social service activities. The declaration states higher Education should reinforce its role of service to society, especially assisting in the elimination of poverty, intolerance, violence, illiteracy, lounger, environmental degradation and disease.

- The **National Policy on Education** has laid considerable emphasis on value education by highlighting the need to make education a powerful tool for cultivation of social and moral values. Keeping in view the pluralistic base of our society, the education system besides preserving our cultural heritage has also to nurture our youth to be more adaptable to life in the changing environment. An inter-linking of education and culture has also been emphasized in the Programme of action for implementation of National Policy on Education.

- People say that Values cannot be taught but caught. Against this belief educationists strongly advocate that values could be taught with sufficient care and caution. In this regard, The National Council for Educational Research and Training (NCERT)in its publication documents on Social, Moral and Spiritual Values in Education (1979) has drawn up 84 values to be inculcated through education. The cultural values need to be identified for standard curricula all over the country. Respect for the old, care for poor and up-privileged and tolerance should be some of the values. Value based inter-personal relations, importance of racial and religious harmony and concern for humanity should form the basis for friendship and cooperation amongst the people.

Status of Value Education in the Present Curriculum

- For strengthening the unity and integrity of the nation, it is essential that the cultural heritage, traditions and history of the different ethnic groups and regions of the country and their contributions are to be understood and appreciated in the social science curriculum. The teaching of mathematics should enhance the child's resources to think and reason, to visualize and handle abstractions, to formulate and solve problems. The teaching of mathematics in high school and higher secondary level, the standard is seemed to be beyond the ability, capability and potentiality of students. Thereby they hinder the values of reasoning, problem solving abilities of children with stress and strain. This broad spectrum of aims can be covered by teaching relevant and important mathematics embedded in the child's level and experience.
- The teaching of science should be recast so that it enables children to examine and analyze everyday experiences. Concerns and issues pertaining to the environment are not emphasized in every subject and through a Wide range of activities.

- In the social sciences, the approach proposed the National Curriculum Frame work recognizes disciplinary markers while emphasizing integration on significant themes, such as water. A paradigm shift is recommended, proposing the study of the social sciences from the perspective of marginalized groups.

- Many in India are not aware of the progress and achievement and specialty of the country in various fields including science and technology. Strengthening of national identity and unity is to be intimately associated with the study of the cultural heritage of India. School curriculum has just ignored the inclusion of specific content to forge national identity, unity, a profound sense of nationalism and patriotism, non- sectarian attends, capacity for tolerating differences arising out of caste, religion, ideology, region, language, sex, etc. in the entire curriculum, of course those aspects are emphasized at minimum range in the language and social sciences.

- Though a broad spectrum of viewpoints exists in the school curriculum, there should be at least six areas of values where teachers need to work in order for the democracy to continue to exist.
    - The need for participation
    - The worth of and rights of the individual
    - The rule of the majority and the rights of the minority
    - Personal responsibility
    - Respect for law and authority and for other people
    - Equality and justice

- In order to reshape the present curriculum that is embedded with necessary 4 values, teachers and educationists must have a vision on the whole approach of the present curriculum. Fine arts, music, creative writing, analytical thinking are not given due place in the curricula right from school to the university level. The curriculum should strike a balance between theory and practice. Creative work in fields of music, dance, literatu.re, drama, visual arts is essential to cultivate the inherent tolerance of children. Value education should be thought as a compulsory subject up to the high school level. It should be made an examinable subject at the school level. Evaluation of value education should be based on compassion, self-reliance, respect and honesty. 'Language teachers should be sensitive towards teaching the content with commitment since language is an important medium for inculcating, fostering and propagating of moral values and national cultural heritage.

- Present curriculum seems not to be helpful in cultivating self-knowledge, self-confidence, self-sacrifice and self-realization of the students. Of course curriculum involves cognitive, affective and psychomotor domains. But the values of knowledge and practice of healthy living, growth and development in self-direction and better human relationship is not at all focused.

- Ultimately the status of value education in the curriculum depends upon the way in that teachers implement the suggestion recommended by Kothari commission given as early as 1964-66. The commission observed the teaching of values should be done both by direct and indirect manner in building a good character. The consciousness of value must permeate the whole curriculum through the subjects taught in different classes. Starting with secondary level emphasis is given to the good behaviour at home leading to good behavior at school, forgiveness, cleanliness, hospitality, helpfulness and loving nature, original. Approach, love for games, simplicity, integrity, obedience, friendliness, good habits and seeking God.

- Curriculum significance must be given to the values such as discipline, good behavior, patience, humility, confidence duty, motivation, harmonious living, accepting mistakes, empathy, comforting words, joy, listening, lover coming obstacles and playing.

- The emphasis is given to the following values namely obedience, gratitude, sharing, punctuality, serving attitude, brotherhood, flexibility, satisfaction, responsibility, keeping up the promises, charity, moving with other students, caring physical health, food habits, self-confidence and knowing oneself. Knowing about winners in different fields intrinsically inculcates self-esteem.

- Social customs as values are integrated into languages and social sciences besides other subjects of learning to such extent that they are integrated into the characteristics of our children

  - Use of literary quotes and linguistic fluency in natural Tamil expressions.

  - Communicative skills to read simple English texts such as news items and write essential letters and convey important information.

  - Logical thinking through codification and symbolization and solve simple problems arising around them.

  - Scientific spirits-observe, collect and analyze objects around to evolve commonness in them for purposes of classification.

  - Social justice through the study of cultural development over the ages, spread of geographical features over the country's landscape, essential citizenship characteristics and economic considerations in all the activities.

  - Computer skills to search for the required information in understanding the subjects learnt.

- Awareness of healthcare and prevention of diseases and develop physical agility and mental alertness in school life and later.

- At the high school level, the above mentioned values in the previous classes, seemed to have importance to the following values, they are purposefulness, culture, empathy, hard work, unity, saving attitude , and development of reading habits.

- The curriculum should focuses on awareness, creativity, unique qualities, good leadership, accountability, realizing and fulfilling the objects, team performance, decision making, adventurous attitude, respecting others and other genders, 'overcoming failures, excellence etc.,

- Higher secondary school level prepares every individual child in to adolescence. They ought to know about self-control, neutrality, independence, equality, integrity and social duties apart from the values inculcated in their earlier years. They should become aware of the benefit of the moral values of not stealing others ideas.

- As a culmination of inculcation of values, students become associated with self-concept, goal of life, motivation, victories and failures, utilizing opportunities, clarification of evil qualities that are to be taken care of as a "caution".

The status of value education in the curriculum definitely motivates, propels and prompts every learner to modify the behaviour in the desired direction as expected by the educational aims and objectives.

Role of School in Value Education

Morning Assembly

Before starting the teaching work in the school, it is necessary to hold a morning assembly for 15 to 20 minutes. There should be prayer, religious discourses, patriotic songs and moral lectures in the assembly to develop values such as punctuality, faith in god, team spirit, orderliness, patriotism and discipline.

Compulsory Subjects

Moral education should be taught as a compulsory subject. This education should contain the substance of all the religions. At least two periods in a week should be reserved for this subject in the time table.

Extension Lectures of Scholars

National and spiritual leaders should be invited to the institution from time-to-time to express their views on the subjects of human interests.

Skits and Dramas

The subject matter of skits and dramas organized in the school should be moral, society and cultural values.

Use of Mass Media

Maximum use of the mass media should be made to provide value education in the school. The mass Medias such as newspapers, journals, radio and television can be used to develop social, moral and cultural values among the students.

Re-designing the Curriculum

Some changes should be made in the curriculum keeping in the view the social, moral, cultural and notional values. The subjects like history, geography, social studies, science, languages, literature and arts, should be included in the curriculum as they inculcate the values such as cooperation, unselfishness, desire to serve, national spirit, international brotherhood, truthfulness, hospitality, leadership qualities, social justice, sharing, courage, faith in god and serving the poor.

School Magazine

Magazines that are published by the schools should contain articles related to value oriented education. Such magazines enable the students to get value education that develop desirable values in them.

Role of the Teacher in Value Education

The teacher has to play a very important role in the inculcation of value oriented education in the new generation. This is because the twenty-first century has seen remarkable development in science and technology explosion in population and in human desire.

- The teacher must have faith in the basic human values.
- The teacher should cultivate the basic human values in students.
- The teacher should develop faith in democratic, socialistic and secular values.
- The teacher should help in the conservation of environmental resources and preservation of the cultural heritage.
- The teacher should encourage students to organize entrained clubs in the entire state and inter-district.

Objectives of Value Education

- National Policy on Education (1986).
- UNESCO (1980)

National Policy on Education (1986)

It has mentioned the following aims of education based on values such as non-violence, truth, love, cooperation, justice, tolerance, coexistence, democratic and scientific attitude and a healthy critical thinking.

- To develop the physical, mental, intellectual and aesthetic aspects of the individual.
- To inculcate a scientific attitude and create democratic, moral and religious values.
- To develop firm determination for the solution of the problems.
- To make the individual conscious and awakened relating to material, social, technological, economic and cultural environment.
- To develop respect for the individual dignity of labour and a healthy and positive attitude.
- To be dedicated towards the unity and integrity of the country and to provide a firm pace to the development of the country.
- To remain firm on secularism and social justice.
- To develop international understanding.

UNESCO (1980)

- Full development of the child's personality in its physical, mental, emotional and spiritual aspects.
- Inculcation of good manners and creation of responsible and cooperative citizenship.
- Developing a democratic way of thinking and living.

- Enabling children to have faith in some supernatural power and order that is supposed' to control this universe and human life.
- Developing tolerance towards and understanding of different religious faiths.
- Developing a séance of brotherhood at the social, national and international level.
- Inculcation of a spirit of patriotism and national integration.

Role of Students in Value Education

Introspection and Self-Analysis

An inward focusing on mental experiences, such as sensations or feelings. The conscious mental and purposive process relaying on thinking, reasoning and examination of one's own thoughts and perceptions. The process of directly examining one's own conscious mental states and processes. In psychology introspection is a method of inquiry in that subjects attempt to examine the contents and processes of their consciousness. Literally, introspection means "looking inward". Allows people not only to check the validity of their mental processes in terms of their accuracy, but also their moral or ethical status. The introspective ability is an essential balance to our free will, allowing us the opportunity to check our thoughts and plans and thus to be responsible for them.

Helps ensure that our actions and behaviors are consistent with our fundamental selves, our personal truths and serves to bolster self-confidence and self-assurance and the vibrating frequency of our own energy. Periodic introspection as a purposeful process is an important and necessary activity for us as leaders because it keeps us centered, energized and balanced.

"Who looks outside dreams, who looks inside awakes"

Carl Gustav Jung

Character Formation

Character is a psychological notion that refers to all the habitual ways of feeling and reacting that distinguish one individual from another. Sigmund Freud had a sustained interest in the question of character formation, since it touches on the major themes. In The Interpretation of Dreams (1900), Freud defined character in relationship to the unconscious and describe as our character is based on the memory-traces of our impression and moreover the impressions that have had the greatest effect on us those of our earliest youth are precisely the ones and scarcely ever become conscious. Five years later, in Three Essays on the Theory of sexuality, Freud emphasized individual psychic activity and described as a person's character is built up to a considerable extent from the material of sexual excitations and is composed of instincts that have been fixed since childhood, or constructions achieved by means of sublimation, and of other constructions, employed for effectively holding in check perverse impulses that have been recognized as being utilizable.

Obstinacy, thrift and orderliness arise from an exploitation of anal egotism, while ambition is determined by a strong urethral-erotic component. Character derives from instincts, but not directly, since reaction formations and sublimations intervene. With the development of the notion of identification, that of character took on additional dimensions. Character formation was understood to be based on the mechanism of identification that is unconsciously identifying with character traits derived from objects.

The notion of character thus evolved in Freud's work. The importance Freud attributed to it can be seen in his remarks in "Freud's Psycho-Analytic Procedure and written as Deep-rooted malformations of character, traits of an actually degenerate constitution. Some Character-types met with in Psycho-Analytic Work", Freud noted that it is not the character traits that patients see in them, nor those attributed to patients by persons close to them that pose the greatest problem for analysts, rather it is the previously unknown and surprising peculiarities often revealed in the course of analysis. Freud analyzed some of the character types revealed through analysis, including those of subjects who claim for themselves the right to perpetrate injustice because they believe they have been subjected to it themselves, subjects "wrecked by success" and finally, taking a perspective that changed criminology, "criminals from a sense of guilt".

A broader, more central notion of character can be found in the work of Wilhelm Reich. The idea of character analysis, and especially that of "character armor," is linked to his theories of a biological energy that he later named "orgone energy." Subsequently, these theories became a separate discipline from psychoanalysis, "bioenergy." character types (hysterical, obsessional, masochistic, etc.) under the presupposition that the primordial function of any character type is to defend against stimulations from the external world and against repressed internal instincts. The character analysis he developed consists in isolating in the patient the character trait that is the source of greatest resistance and thus rendering it analyzable. Thus, character is essentially a mechanism of narcissistic protection hence the term "character armor."

Character Plays an Essential Role in Personality Development

Remember personality development is not only about looking good and wearing expensive brands. It is also about developing one's inner self and being a good human being. An individual is nervous only when he is ashamed of what is doing. Character is something that an individual is born with and seldom changes with time as against behaviour. Honesty is an individual's inherent character that would never change irrespective of his/her situation or circumstance.

Character includes traits such as

- Honesty
- Leadership
- Trust
- Courage
- Patience

CHAPTER III

SOURCES OF VALUES AND WAYS OF TEACHING VALUES

Sources of Values

As a system, values are the set of meta-physical beliefs about man and his life. And so it is derived as a relationship between a person and the situation that evokes an appreciative response in the individual. These values can be caught from different sources such as socio-cultural tradition, religion and constitution.

Socio-Cultural Tradition

Values are expressions of emotionalized truths that implemented energize whatever they come in contact with, enabling the greatest positive results with the least effort in the shortest period of time, whether it is for the individual, a collective, or society as a whole. Society acquires values through a long process of trial and error experimentation with various approaches to life. Over years and centuries, the collective comes to recognize that certain principles, or guidelines are essential for the survival or vital for the growth of the individual and the community. They learn from different sources like socio-cultural tradition to signify these essential principles and pass them on to future generations as guidelines for action. In ancient Indian system, there was a special effort for nourishment of the good values through the educational system itself.

The culture of a society is the way of life of its members, the collection of ideas and habits that they learn, share and transmit from generation to generation. Since human beings have no instinct to direct their actions, their behavior must be based on guidelines that are learned. But for a society to operate effectively, these guidelines must be shared by its members. Culture therefore has two essential qualities to be learned and shared. Without it there would be no human society. Culture defines accepted ways of behaving for members of a particular society. Such definitions vary from society to society.

Culture means the development and growth of ancient customs, behavioral patterns, lifestyle, habits, values of life, religious beliefs, principles, spiritual knowledge, and creation of art and literature of particular group of people and is passed on from generation to generation. Indian culture is rich and diverse. It has attained a prominent place among all the cultures of the world. Their customs, manners, way of communicating with one another, these all are one of the important components of Indian culture. Even though Indians have accepted modern means of living, they have improved their living standard but their values and beliefs still remain unchanged. A modern Indian can change his way of clothing, way of eating and living but the rich values in a person always remain unchanged because they are deeply rooted within their hearts, mind, body and soul that they receive from their culture. Every culture has a set of moral and social values. Some cultures or societies change faster than others, but there is a stability found in a common set of values. Indian culture is rich and diverse and as a result unique in its very own way. Hospitality, respecting one another, helping, tendency, care and sacrifice, humanity, tolerance, unity, secularism, spirituality and problem solving are greatly valued in our culture.

Hospitality: Indian culture treats guests as God and serves them and takes care of them as if they are a part and parcel of the family itself. "Scripture also enjoins that one should treat visiting enemies so well that they will forget their animosity. A graphic example is that of the warrior class who would fight during the day and in the evening socializes with adversaries. Westerners visiting India and other places in the East are often astonished by the welcoming attitude towards guests and visiting strangers, strikingly different from the Western 'beware of the dog' culture. The youngsters give lots of respect to the elders. Elders are considered to be the head of the family and have the control of the family in their hands. The elders give blessings to the youngsters when the youngsters touch their feet.

Respect One Another: 'Elders and the respect for elders' is a great value of Indian culture. Elders are the driving force for any family and hence the love and respect for elders comes from within and is not artificial. An individual takes blessings from his elders by touching their feet. It is a land of aspirations, achievements and self- reliance. All people are alike and respecting one another. Elders pass on this culture to next generation as we enter into it. India has also the birthplace of many religions such as Hinduism, Sikhism, Jainism, Buddhism and many more are there. The various traditions that are formed by these amalgamations have influenced the other parts of the world too. There is an important lesson that is being taught in India, it is to give complete "Respect to one another". There is no discrimination made among the people, all are considered to be equal.

Helping Tendency: Helpfulness is the chief feature of Indian culture. People are ready to help each other when one is in need and is in distress. The help might not be in monetary terms, it can also be forwarded in non-monetary ways also. Here the people believe in distributing happiness and sharing pain. By these methods people develop a strong bonding reflecting Indian values. Helpful nature is another striking feature in our Indian culture. It tells us that by all this we can develop cooperation and better living amongst ourselves and subsequently make this world a better place to live in.

Care and Sacrifice: The values of care and sacrifice are cherished from our Indian culture. The family is the most important institution that has survived through the ages. Family is the foundation stone of society, modifies individual behaviors and cultivates tolerance, patience, respect for others, love and affection, dedication, care and sacrifice. Family is about joy and sharing. The family culture is all about love and patience. Families are also getting nuclear owing to independent lifestyle preference and also the concept wherein both husband and wife are working and have demanding careers. The earlier homes housed themselves together in very large families where one can actually see three or four generations put up together.

Humanity: India's spiritual, culture and civilization have ever served to enlighten humanity. The Indians are noted for their humanness and calm nature without any harshness in their principles and ideals. The mildness of the Indians has continued till date, despite the aggressiveness of the Muslim conquerors and the reforming zeal of the British, the Portuguese and the Dutch.

Tolerance: As a nation of so many cultures, India is very unique in several ways. It might be argued that tolerance to circumstances or situations that one finds themselves in, is very common to people of different nations. Still there are several unique characteristics of this tolerance, and this has huge economic dimensions as well.

Unity: 'Unity in Diversity' has been the distinctive feature of our culture. To live peacefully has been our motto and this motto has helped us to achieve Independence. In our struggle for freedom people from different communities participated, keeping one thing in mind that they all are Indians first It is a fusion of old traditional values and the modern principles, thus satisfying all the three generations in the present India. The culture of India has been shaped by the long history of India, its unique geography and the absorption of customs, traditions and ideas from some of its neighbors as well as by preserving its ancient heritages, that were formed during the Indus Valley Civilization and evolved further during the Vedic age, rise and decline of Buddhism, Golden age, Muslim conquests and European colonization. India does not have a strong uniform national culture. India's great diversity of cultural practices, languages, customs, and traditions are examples of this unique. Most Indians emphasize the country's cultural diversity, tolerance of difference, and receptiveness to foreign influences.

Secularism: As India is a secular country, our culture also exhibits and stresses on Secularism. There is freedom of worship throughout the length and breadth of India without any breeches or violations of any other's religious beliefs. The catholicity of the Indian culture can be best understood by the fact that hundreds of Hindus visit the Velankanni shrine or the Nagore Dargah in Tamilnadu.

Spirituality: India is a nation that is one of the cradles of civilization -5000 years old. Many of our traditions descended from Vedic times. Although most of us believe that are made by ourselves somewhere deep within us are roots that have actually contributed in some way. Traditions and sacraments practiced are unchanged and, an understanding of the shlokas/mantras, or propitiation of our Gods will help us understand ourselves and, our cultural roots. Marriage traditions in India among most communities, be they Hindu, Sikh, or Jain, come down from Vedic times and incorporate several social customs that are peculiar to a region or community. Weddings at one time were elaborate affairs of ten days today, most wedding are planned over two day or sometimes just a day.

The most of the spiritual values are cherished from the Upanishads are Hindu scriptures. The Upanishads are not just abstract philosophies. They can be used in day-to-day life to find one's true purpose in life and achieve everlasting joy. The Upanishads are the holy books of the Hindus. In their verses lies the spiritual and philosophical backbone of Hinduism. Some call the Upanishads 'Vedanta', that means that the Upanishads represent the ultimate culmination of the Vedas.

The Upanishads are Hindu scriptures that discuss the nature of God, reality, and the individual soul. The most important Upanishad of Katha. Upanishad compares the individual body to a chariot driven by senses-instead of horses. Our goals are the roads. The individual soul is said to be the master of this chariot, the intellect the charioteer, and the mind the reins. When an individual has a restrained mind, firmly holding the reins, he reaches the end of the road self-realization. Another chief Upanishad of Mundaka Upanishad teaches us about the truth. India's famous motto 'Satyameva Jayate' (truth alone prevails) is actually taken from this Upanishad.

Problem Solving: One has to transform such knowledge to wisdom by applying the principles and core values in one's life. The Ramayana describes the epic battle to wipe out Evil. It not only teaches us dharma, but also sheds light on the human predicament and the choices that lie before us. It teaches us that problems are inevitable in one's life, but if one is filled with wisdom and devotion one can overcome any problem. There is an elaborating unique message inherent in Ramayana. It deals with various topics like administration, business management, communication skills, and tips to success and family living.

The Indian society of today largely derives its values and attitude to life and the world from the cultural framework suggested in the older scriptures. The basic values of any society continue to be freedom and liberty, these are echoed in our constitution as well. Indians as a people are tolerant, accommodating, open-minded and spiritual and accept religious differences. The strength of a society lies in the values not just upheld in the political documents, but in the values upheld by individual members. For over 4000 years our culture has been enriched and denuded in some ways however our core values continue to remain the same. Values are the guidelines that each society lives by. Learning about the values of each group of people helps us to understand them as people. One should be able to analyze their responses to situations and people. There is greater harmony among people and it is far easier to build rapport with one another.

Religion

Edward Tyler rightly said that religion is the faith in the spiritual power. Religion, if rightly understood and practiced, need not become a negative factor in national rejuvenation. Religion is nothing but the continuation of the scientific search of truth, at the higher aesthetic, ethical and spiritual levels. Research based on reason has much to offer to humanity. Thus, Religion is primarily concerned with the ethical and moral values. Religious rituals are not usually considered while discussing values. There is naturally a close connection between the values of any tradition and its underlying beliefs or concepts.

Hinduism

Some of the primary teachings of Hinduism contain elaborate explanations of the essence of life. Our relationship with the lower forms like insects, plants and animals, who is God Almighty, how is big bang created, The importance of meditation and yoga, practicing absolute celibacy, traveling the path of absolute truthfulness is a soul "atma", relationship between a soul atma and God almighty etc. are some of the queries the answers to that can-be found in Bhagavad Gita.

Central Values in Hinduism

The most fundamental of the eternal values can be classified into these three disciplines:

1. **Self-control(Brahmachariyam)-** and self-regulation of all physical activities
2. **Non-injury(Ahimsa)-** self-regulation of all mental activities.

3. **Truthfulness (Satyain)**- self-regulation of all 'intellectual activities.

- **Self-control(Brahmachariyam):** According to Hinduism Brahmacharya gives good health, inner strength, peace of mind and long life. It invigorates the mind and nerves. It helps to conserve physical and mental energy. It augments memory and will force brain power. It bestows tremendous strength, vigor and vitality. Strength and fortitude are obtained.

- **Non-injury (Ahimsa):** According to Hinduism, Ahimsa is certainly not cowardice, it is wisdom. And wisdom is the cumulative knowledge of the existing divine laws of reincarnation, karma, and dharma, the all pervasiveness and sacredness of things, blended together within the psyche or soul of the Hindu. Hindus do not substantially differentiate the soul within a human body from that of an animal.

- **Self-regulation (Truthfulness):** Self-control is necessary for any spiritual progress. Unruly thoughts, attractions of the senses, lustful desires, anger, covetousness and avarice constantly arise in the mind of the person who has no mental discipline, and these impel him to do evil deeds. If a person cannot direct his thoughts, desires, and actions according to his own will, how can he possibly direct his soul to God and keep his life on the path of truth? Unless the higher mind is strengthened and given the willpower to master the impulses of the flesh mind, there will be little room for God to dwell in that mind.

- **Love:** Be compassionate towards all living beings, thus love all living beings. This means don't be envious or hateful of others. Be friendly to others, be nice to others, be kind to others, be generous to others, be merciful to others, and be charitable to the needy.

- **Satisfaction:** Satisfaction means that one should not be eager to gather more and more material goods by unnecessary activity. One should be satisfied with the things obtained by the grace of the Supreme Lord that is called satisfaction. Tapas means austerity or penance. There are many rules and regulations in the Vedas sometimes it is very troublesome to rise early in the morning, but whatever voluntary trouble one may suffer in this way is called penance.

Christianity

Based on the birth of Jesus, history is divided in to BC and AD. To any one, Christianity means Ten Commandments.

- Blessed and enviably happy.
- Blessed
- Blessed and fortunate and. happy and spiritually prosperous
- Blessed (happy, to be envied, and spiritually prosperous with life-joy and satisfaction in Gods favor and salvation-regardless of their outward conditions) are the merciful, for they shall obtain mercy!
- Blessed(happy, enviably fortunate and spiritually prosperous possessing the happiness produced by the experience of Gods favor and especially conditioned by the revelation of His grace, regardless of their outward conditions) are the pure in heart, for they shall see God!

The word of 'God written in the Holy Bible is so precious because man shall not live by bread alone the power of Resurrection is the secret of victory over sin. Thus Christianity is nothing but love in action as given in I. Corinthians 13th chapter verses 1-13.

- It does not dishonor others, it is not self-seeking, it is not easily angered, it keeps no record of wrongs.
- Love does not delight in evil but rejoices with the truth. It always protects, always trusts, always hopes, and always perseveres.
- Love never fails. But where there "are prophecies, they will cease, where there are tongues, they will be stilled, where there is knowledge, it will pass away.

Islam

The religion of Islam is based on the foundations of love, respect, devotion and happiness. Islam stresses strong connections in between fellow human beings, between the body and soul and most important of all, the bond between man and his creator, the Almighty God.

- **Truthfulness:** According to Islam religion, truthfulness is an essential attribute of every single prophet who graced the earth. Truthfulness is something that is to be cultivated till it becomes implanted in a person's soul and disposition and therefore reflected throughout the person's character.
- **Sincerity and Purity**: sincerity is one of the most significant qualities of those most faithful or loyal to Allah, loyalty is regarded as a source, and sincerity as sweet water originating from it. Loyalty or faithfulness is the primary attribute of Prophet Hood, and sincerity is its most lustrous dimension. Sincerity is innate in the prophets all other people try to obtain it during their lifetime.

Buddhism

The potable feature of the Buddhism is the absence of a personal Creator or God in its tenets. Buddha did not deny the existence of God and preached that the universe is guided and governed by a Supreme Power that did not possess a name or form. Consequently, all rites and rituals became defunct. The core of his teaching consists of the four noble truths, followed by the eight-fold path. The four noble truths are as follows:

- The world is full of suffering and sorrow.
- The cause of suffering is desire.
- The renunciation of desires will lead to salvation from
- the world, and
- The path to salvation can be achieved by following The Eight-Fold Path.

The Eight-Fold Paths are:

- Right Knowledge 4 means a basic and thorough understanding of the Four Noble Truths.
- Right Attitude means having an unselfish and mentally healthy attitude to life, free from hatred and covetousness.
- Right Speech means speaking words that are good and true. One should not lie or gossip.
- Right Action means always conducting oneself in a way that does not harm, hurt nor displease anyone. Adultery, cheating, stealing and murder are specifically denounced.
- Right Means of Livelihood means that one must always strive to earn to earn one's livelihood by honest means.
- Right Effort means one should conscientiously strive to develop well tendencies and destroy negative inclinations.

- Right Awareness means we should introspect about our inclinations and not give in easily to temptation.

- Right Meditation means working towards training your mind towards intense concentration in turn, will lead to salvation.

Jainism

Lord Mahavir did not ascribe to idea of a God as the ultimate creator, protector and destroyer. He did not believe that ritualistic idol worship would put the human soul on the road to salvation. He believed that when a living being destroys all his karmas, he possesses perfect knowledge, vision, power, and bliss. He becomes omniscient and omnipotent. This living being becomes a God according to Jain religion. Hence Jains do not believe in one God. Gods in Jain religion are innumerable and the number is continuously increasing as more living beings attain liberation. Every living being has a potential to become God of the Jain religion.

- Universal love

- Non-violence

- Triple gems of Jainism

- Celibacy (Bramachariyam)

- Non-materialism

- Truthfulness

- Non-stealing

A religion teaches and preaches values, almost all religions stress on essence of life, truthfulness, peace, love and respect etc., so it is in our hand to foster these values among our children by using religion as a spiritual path. It is also believed that religious hopes, beliefs in a right path will prevent human being from indulging and practicing disvalues such as stealing, lying, dishonest, irregular, disrespect, unkindness etc.

Religion is to do right. It is to love, it is to serve, it is to think and it is to be humble. So religion is a best source to cultivate and practice values.

Constitution

The cherished values of the constitution are enshrined in the great words of its preamble. The values of the nation of India, expressed in the preamble to the constitution, area modern set of values in step with the universal declaration of human rights.

- JUSTICE, social, economic and political.
- LIBERTY of thought, expression, belief, faith and worship.
- EQUALITY of status and of opportunity, and to promote among them all
- FRATERNITY assuring the dignity of the individual and the unity and integrity of the Nation.

The Universal Declaration of Human Rights: "Education shall be directed to the full development of the human personality and to the strengthening of respect for human rights and fundamental freedoms. It shall promote understanding, tolerance and friendship among all nations, racial or religious groups and shall further the activities of the United Nations for the maintenance of peace". The Declaration also recommends that a culture of peace be fostered through education by ensuring that children benefit from education on the values, attitudes, modes of behaviour and ways of life enabling them to resolve disputes peacefully instilling in them the values and goals of a culture of peace.

Our constitution promises justice, social, economic and political, Liberty of thought, expression, belief, freedom of faith and Worship, Equality of status and opportunity and to promote fraternity, assuring the dignity of the individual and the unity and integrity of the nation. Positive and constructive citizenship is the backbone of any country. Fundamental values of citizenship a constitution can be explained as follows

- To use their valuable voting rights freely and properly to elect truthful and good character representatives who are committed to their party manifesto and active cooperation in public works.

- To make policies and take decision for wellbeing of the people and help in creating consensus. Representatives should respect and tolerate different views and options.

- Indian Constitution that have following values of Citizenship.

- To promote the spirit of inquiry, scientific outlook, humanism and reform.

- To abide by the constitution and respect its ideals and institutions, the National flag and National Anthem.

- To sustain and protect unity amongst diverse people of India within a common bond of Constitutional Justice on the ideals of liberty, equality, fraternity and justice.

- To value and preserve the rich heritage of our composite culture, to defend and improve the natural environment including forest, lakes, rivers and wildlife and to have compassion for living.

- To strive towards excellence in all spheres of individual and collective activity so that the nation constantly rise to higher levels of endeavour and achievement.

No law can be enacted or amended in a manner that violates the spirit of the preamble. World, free from all the bias and inequality, after all the constitution is for the people, of the people and by the people of this nation. Our constitution makers had indeed made a bold, experiment when they created the constitution in the backdrop of the society that prevails, in our country. Education without values is waste of money, energy and time. True education should train Head and Heart of the man for all round development. As Theodore Roosevelt said that man who has never gone to school may steal from a freight car, but be has a university education, be may steal the whole railroad'. So, educating the mind without values creates a maniac in society. There should be education along with moral values. Students must not only be taught academic subjects in school, but moral values and ethics as well. People must stop confining themselves to the often narrow limits of religion and embrace a wider spiritual outlook. Teachers should appreciably teach values from our socio cultural traditional facts and from constitution that instruct and guide us to live with well-defined values.

How to Teach Values

No method suits in all the situations as there are individual differences even twins differ, teachers also differ Human behaviour is guided by values, that cover cognitive, affective and psychomotor domains, acquired by examples transmitted (caught) by that people do. A child is provided with many choices and allowed to take own decision. A good teacher reflects values rather than impose them on a child.

It is really a problem for teacher to teach values. Teaching is an art and methods are the way to comprehend and practice this art. No method suits in all situations. As there are individual differences, teachers also differ in their personality and children differ in consideration to their families, locality, spiritual, mental and physical development and the teaching method is largely affected by the milieu of the teacher and the pupil.

There are three methods/approaches for teaching and inculcating values and teachers may select from them in accordance with the needs.

a) Direct method/approach

b) Indirect method/ approach

c) Integrated method/approach

Direct Method / Approaches

They aim at teaching of values by setting apart a period every day for each class. There are five major techniques that are as follows.

- Silent Sitting (Turning in)
- Prayers
- Group Singing
- Storytelling
- Group Activities

Silent Sitting

Silent sitting means conditions of being quiet, absence of sound and not speaking. Various education commissions like for University Education Commission(1948-49) suggested for practical silent meditation in the common hall or classroom every day and also recommended at the higher education level these Words. Silent mediation a short period of silent worship or mediation before the class work starts should become an integral part of college life. For a few moments we may free the mind from the distraction of daily living and the forces that determine the meaning and value of life. The spirit of man is candle of lord. In depth silence the voice of God can be heard of Silence is more effective food in helping the child free goodness and beauty. Prayer, gives them work and more strength.

Prayers

Prayer lifts the consciousness from lower selfish desire to heights of noble aspirations. It gives a strong positive outlook to life situation and ourselves.

There are three types of prayers:

- Stutiior strotras (chanted in praise of the God)
- Praarthana or supplication (asking for favors of protection, guidance, begging an apology)
- Subhasitani or expression of (noble thoughts or feelings)

Techniques of School Prayers

All school should starts with the morning assembly and daily prayer. Prayer reveals the essential unity of all faiths. It may be sung with music if possible. Full care should be taken of proper pronunciation and correct rhythm. For new prayer and its introduction, the teacher should explain the meaning and its importance. The value of prayer in daily life full of virtues should be made to be realized. After ending of the prayer students should be asked to do 2-3 minutes of silent sitting for better comprehension of the meaning of prayer and preached to reflect on the day-to-day behavior.

Group Singing

Music is the language of feelings at the heart having universal appeal. All children love music and singing, and singing in group provides more pleasures. A series of lectures even may fail to make an impact, while a single melodious song may touch and melt the heart of any individual.

The music and singing acts as an effective teaching device for Value Education. A number experimental and research studies have proved that group singing, accompanied rhythm and music, can improve the learning ability of slow learners and emotional adjustment of the maladjusted students. Swami Vivekananda said the sounds that emerge out of pure feelings spread 'all through the atmosphere around us. These sound vibrations reach the furthest possible distances in space and leave an exhilarating effect on the heart and soul of those who breathe them.

Storytelling

Storytelling is meant to inculcate or make faith strong. The Puranas and Upanishads are full of stories. They are based on the human values like truth, righteousness, good conduct, love and non-violence and they are highly effective for value teaching. Stories of great persons lives inspire the listeners for value realization. The success of the storytelling depends upon a number of factors:

1. Selection of stories

2. Presentation of stories

a) Narration   c) Dramatization

b) Picturization   d) Questioning

Selection of Stories

- Selection of proper and relevant stories is important.
- The selection should be made according to the interest of listeners.
- They may be taken from a) Religious text b) Folk love c) Mythology d) Lives of great personalities e) Literature.
- The theme should be selected keeping in mind the age group of the listeners and the values to inculcate.
- The story must be simple and easy to identify the characters.

Presentation of Stories

Stories can be presented by proper narration and can be made more appealing through dramatization and picturisation as effective tool in helping the child to see goodness and beauty. The daily practice of prayer helps in increasing their power of concentration. It helps in building a strong will to accept the challenges of life.

Narration

Narration is an art that includes proper movements, gestures, modulation of voices, punctuation, pauses, facial expression tone and stress that directly touch the hearts of listeners. Greater truths and higher values of life will unfold on their own, slowly as the child grows up and as the time passes. The narrators tell the story, comprehending all the mysterious aspects.

Picturisation

Stories demonstrated through pictures or slides are more effective and successful than narration. The stories in picture

- Must be clear.
- Must be bright.
- Must depict only the major parts of the story.
- Should be shown in sequential order.

Dramatization

The best impact on the student is, provided through the dramatization. It does not necessarily involve scenery or costumes or background music like theatre, rather it is just a role-play or delivery of dialogue by different students. It is a well-known fact of psychology and children are imitators. Hence they should be provided with ample opportunities to improve their actions, explain their thoughts through postures etc. of their own.

Questioning

Questioning follows after story narration, picturisation and dramatization. The question can be

- Factual/ Confirmative.
- For comprehension.
- To know home application skills.

- For ability to evaluation.
- For ability to criticizes.
- For developing the power of imagination.
- For fostering creativity.

Group Activities

Group activities are those activities that are carried out by the students in a group situation. Group activities for Value Education may be as follows:

- Role-play
- Dealing with value dilemmas
- Special projects and exhibitions
- Special work and self-reliance activities
- Watching good films, videos, documentaries, and
- Discussion activities.

Role-Play

Role-Play is a feedback device for modification of behavior, in that participants assume an identity of other persons and then react as they perceive their behavior in a particular set of circumstances. This opportunity helps the child to get insight into mind of other person and enlarges his social vision, develops the values of sympathy, kindness and sensitivities to others perceptions, feelings and imitation of social relations.

Community Survey

- Health and Sanitation campaigns special in slum areas.
- Participation in community development activities like construction of Wells, ponds, tanks, roads, public buildings, social forestry etc.
- Hospital visits to serve the sick people.
- Distribution of food and clothes to poor and needy persons.
- Social services during community and national festivals.

- Organizing cultural programmes in the community.
- Each education institution should organize such activities that promote self-reliance among students. They may be of the following forms:
    - Campus beautification.
    - Maintenance of "school plant.
    - Leveling playground.
    - Whitewashing, painting and decorating classrooms.
    - Carrying out minor repairs of school equipment.
    - Running a cooperative sale counter for students.

Watching Films, Videos and Documentaries

A large numbers of films, video cassettes and documentaries, have been utilized by every school for enriching the values of students' teaching-learning process.

The State Institutes of Educational Technology (SIET) produced a number of programmes for broadcasting clear messages for education in values like environmental protection, perversion of natures, animal care, health and physical fitness, family welfare etc. The documentaries on cultural aspects, cultural festivals, care of historical monuments and classical dances etc. also inculcate values.

- These should follow systematic procedure.
- The resources should be properly used.
- After presentation, students should be engaged to explore, comprehend and valuate the inherent values in the programme.
- Students should be encouraged to follow up activities like community service, dramatization, further self-study etc.
- Student should be enabled to assimilate internalize and practice the values.

Indirect Approaches/Methods

Apart from direct method, values can also be inculcated by indirect approach. This approach includes incidental approach and contrived or planned approach.

Incidental Approach

In the teaching and learning process, value inculcation may be possible with an unexpected incident i.e. of the playfields or outside classroom. It is a deliberate and conscious effort.

Suppose two students have quarreled on the playfield and one is injured. After treating the injured, the teacher may ask for the cause of the incident. Side by side the teacher may explain the evil effects of and also teach about non-violence. Thus, it is called incidental approach.

Contrived or Planned Approach

In contrived approach the teacher can deliberately think upon such desirable values that may be developed during various stages of planned activities. When a teacher is organizing an excursion, the value of spirit of inquiry can easily emerge to surface because students are very inquisitive about various things during an excursion. .

In planning, the students may work in close cooperation.

In execution, they may emphasize punctuality, cleanliness, economy of time and expenditure, aesthetic value, love of music etc. These may be deliberately planned.

The teacher should observe and evaluate the students for adopting and violating of the values.

Integrated Approach

The integrated approach aims at inculcating the values through all academic programmes and activities. This is practiced through curricular and co-curricular activities.

- Integration of values in curricular work.
- Integration of values in co-curricular activities.

Integration of Values in Curricular Work

In all classroom subjects, languages, mathematics, science, social science and other significant values are implicated in various topics. The school subjects and their values are shown in the table.

Subject	Values	Subject	Values
Mathematics	Rationality	**History**	Partriotism
	Logistic		Tolerance
	Accuracy		Courtesy
Language	Honesty		Courage
	Sensitivity		Patience
	Courtesy		Social service
	Compassion		Heroism
	Obedience		Leadership
	Cheerfulness		Love of cultural
	National Consciousness		Heritage
	Acceptance		Sympathy
	Self-Control		Secularism
	Aesthetic sense		Common cause
	Sprit of inquiry		Humanism
	Citizenship		Belongingness
	Friendship		Social justice
	Ownership	**Geography**	Endurance
General Science	Rationality		Unity in diversity
	Sensitivity		Interdependence of man
	Observation		Reservation of nature
	Truths fullness	**Environment**	Harmony with nature
	Stability		Love for vegetable and animal kingdom
	Orderliness		Sensitive towards
	Open-mindedness		environmental issues and problems
	Reverence for life in all its forms		Love of animals, birds, etc.
	Self – control		
	Accuracy		

Integration of Values in Co-curricular Activities

The scope of integration of values in co-curricular activities extend even outside the classroom, such as debate, discussion, symposia, drama, games and so on. Activities like student self-government, clubs and associations organized with special interests activities like N.C.C., N.S.S. Boy Scout, Bulbuls, funfair, Red Cross, excursion, fieldtrips, social service community activities, sports, games, cultural activities etc. provide ample opportunities for boys and girls to come together in pursuit of the common goals and ideals. A few activities that may be possibly being organized in schools are given below.

- Morning assembly
- Wall magazine
- Unity thought of the day
- Library reading
- Sports and games
- Drama
- Wall quotes
- Development of beauty spot
- School garden
- Declamation
- Pageants
- Eco-clubs

CHAPTER IV

ETHICS IN PERSONAL AND PROFESSIONAL DEVELOPMENT

Personal Development

Personal Development is a lifelong process. It's a way for people to assess their skills and qualities, consider their aims in life and set goals in order to realize and maximize their potential.

Definition

The process of improving oneself through such activities as enhancing employment skills, increasing consciousness and building wealth. The growing success of the self-help and personal development movement has assisted many business managers in obtaining more qualified and motivated personnel for their companies, and it has also encouraged more people to go into business for themselves.

Personal Development covers activities that improve awareness and identity, develop talents and potential, build human capital and facilitate employability, enhance quality of life and contribute to the realization of dreams and aspirations. When personal development takes place in the context of institutions, it refers to the methods, programs, tools, techniques, and assessment systems that support human development at the individual level in organizations.

Personal development may include the following activities:

- improving self-awareness
- improving self-knowledge
- improving skills or learning new ones
- building or renewing identity/self-esteem
- developing strengths or talents

- improving wealth

- spiritual development

- identifying or improving potential

- building employability or (alternatively) human capital

- enhancing lifestyle or the quality of life

- improving health

- fulfilling aspirations

- initiating a life enterprise or (alternatively) personal autonomy

- defining and executing personal development plans (PDPs)

- improving social abilities

Principle of Personal Development

- Human nature that has been shaped by evolution and has helped humans adapt to their environment.

- People differ from each other in dispositional traits, broad and relatively stable dimensions of personality. Humans differ in their thinking, feeling and behavior.

- Also differ in characteristic adaptations, more situation-specific and changeable ways in people adapt to their roles and environments, including motives, goals, plans, schemas, self-conceptions, stage-specific concerns, and coping mechanisms.

- Differ in narrative identities, unique and integrative "life stories" that we construct about our pasts and futures to give ourselves an identity and our lives meaning.

Ethical Conduct toward Students

The professional educator accepts personal responsibility for teaching students character qualities that will help them evaluate the consequences of and accept the responsibility for their actions and choices. It affirms parents as the primary moral educators of their children. Nevertheless, all educators are obligated to help foster civic virtues such as integrity, diligence, responsibility, cooperation, loyalty, fidelity, and respect-for the law, for human life, for others and for self.

The professional educator, in accepting their position of public trust, measures success not only by the progress of each student toward realization of personal potential, but also as a citizen of the greater community of the republic.

- The professional educator deals considerately and justly with each student, and seeks to resolve problems, including discipline, according to law and school policy.
- The professional educator does not intentionally expose the student to disparagement.
- The professional educator does not reveal confidential information concerning students, unless required by law.
- The professional educator makes a constructive effort to protect the student from conditions detrimental to learning, health or safety.
- The professional educator endeavors to present facts without distortion, bias or personal prejudice.

Ethical Conduct toward Practices and Performance

- The professional educator assumes responsibility and accountability for his or her performance and continually strives to demonstrate competence.

- The professional educator endeavors to maintain the dignity of the profession by respecting and obeying the law, and by demonstrating personal integrity.

- The professional educator applies for, accepts, or assigns a position or a responsibility on the basis of professional qualifications and adheres to the terms of a contract or appointment.

- The professional educator maintains sound mental health, physical stamina, and social prudence necessary to perform the duties of any professional assignment.

- The professional educator continues professional growth.

- The professional educator complies with written local school policies and applicable laws and regulations that are not in conflict with this code of ethics.

- The professional educator does not intentionally misrepresent official policies of the school or educational organizations and clearly distinguishes those views from his or her own personal opinions.

- The professional educator honestly accounts for all funds committed to their charge.

- The professional educator does not use institutional or professional privileges for personal or partisan advantage.

Ethical Conduct toward Parents and Community

- The professional educator pledges to protect public sovereignty over public education and private control of private education.
- The professional educator recognizes that quality education is the common goal of the public, boards of education and educators, and that a cooperative effort is essential among these groups to attain that goal.
- The professional educator makes concerted efforts to communicate to parents all information that should be revealed in the interest of the student.
- The professional educator endeavors to understand and respect the values and traditions of the diverse cultures represented in the community and in his or her classroom.
- The professional educator manifests a positive and active role in school/community relations.

Relational Ethics

The use of relational ethics is critical to work with families. The principles of relational ethics form a basis for understanding specific ethical dilemmas and guide practice first and foremost towards the development of caring and respectful relationships with all family members. Some of the important principles that assist family life educators towards the end are:

1. The parent and family life educator's relationship with individual family members, peers, and the community is both the context and the point of contact for our ethical thinking and actions.
2. Parent and family life educators bear the primary responsibility to initiate a relationship built on trust, caring, and understanding.

3. All relationships have predictable stages of development. Parent and family life educators will adjust their practice to their understanding of the state and stage of a relationship.

4. Parent and family life educators will bring a knowledge base of general principles about children and youth, parenting, family, and community systems to share with family members.

5. Parent and family life educators will set boundaries on their relationships with family members and be responsible for potential negative influences of care taking beyond these limits.

Ethical Principles for Parent and Family Life Educators

- Relationships with Parents and Families
- Relationships with Children and Youth
- Relationships with Colleagues and the Profession
- Relationships with Community/Society

Leadership Quality

Leadership is a holistic spectrum that can arise from:

(1)   Higher levels of physical power, need to display power and control others, force superiority, ability to generate fear, or group-member's need for a powerful group protector (Primal Leadership).

(2)   Superior mental energies, superior motivational forces, perceivable in communication and behaviors, lack of fear, courage, determination (Psycho energetic Leadership).

(3)   Higher abilities in managing the overall picture (Macro-Leadership).

(4)   Higher abilities in specialized tasks (Micro-Leadership).

(5)   Higher ability in managing the execution of a task (Project Leadership), and

(6)   Higher level of values, wisdom, and spirituality.

An **Effective Leader** is generally someone that leads by example and other people just tend to follow because they believe what they do is the right thing.

Personality Development

Personality Development is defined as the relatively enduring pattern of thoughts, feelings, and behaviors that distinguish individuals from one another. The dominant view in the field of personality psychology today holds that personality emerges early and continues to change in meaningful ways throughout the lifespan. Evidence from large-scale, long-term studies has supported this perspective.

Adult personality traits are believed to have a basis in infant temperament, meaning that individual differences in disposition and behavior appear early in life, possibly even before language or conscious self-representation develop. The Five Factor Model of personality has been found to map onto dimensions of childhood temperament, suggesting that individual differences in levels of the "big five" personality traits (neurotic-ism, extraversion, openness to experience, agreeableness, and conscientiousness) are present from young ages.

Five Factors of Personality Development

- **Openness to Experience**: (*inventive/curious* vs. *consistent/cautious*). Appreciation for art, emotion, adventure, unusual ideas, curiosity, and variety of experience. Openness reflects the degree of intellectual curiosity, creativity and a preference for novelty and variety a person has. It is also described as the extent to that a person is imaginative or independent, and depicts a personal preference for a variety of activities over a strict routine.

- **Conscientiousness**:(*efficient/organized* vs. *easy-going/careless*).

  A tendency to be organized and dependable, show self-discipline, act dutifully, aim for achievement, and prefer planned rather than spontaneous behavior. High conscientiousness is often perceived as stubborn and obsessive. Low conscientiousness are flexible and spontaneous, but can be perceived as sloppy and unreliable.

- **Extraversion**:(*outgoing/energetic* vs. *solitary/reserved*).Energy, positive emotions, urgency, assertiveness, sociability and the tendency to seek stimulation in the company of others, and talkativeness. High extraversion is often perceived as attention-seeking, and domineering. Low extraversion causes a reserved, reflective personality that can be perceived as aloof or self-absorbed.

- **Agreeableness**: (*friendly/compassionate* vs. *analytical/detached*).

  A tendency to be compassionate and co-operative rather than suspicious and antagonistic towards others. It is also a measure of one's trusting and helpful nature and whether a person is generally well-tempered or not. High agreeableness is often seen as naive or submissive. Low agreeableness personalities are often competitive or challenging people, that can be seen as argumentative or untrustworthy.

- **Neuroticism**: (*sensitive/nervous* vs. *secure/confident*). The tendency to experience unpleasant emotions easily, such as anger, anxiety, depression, and vulnerability. A high need for stability manifests as a stable and calm personality, but can be seen as uninspiring and unconcerned. A low need for stability causes a reactive and excitable personality, often very dynamic individuals, but they can be perceived as unstable or insecure.

Mass Media and Ethics

Media ethics is the subdivision of applied ethics dealing with the specific ethical principles and standards of media including broadcast media, film, theatre, the arts, print media and the internet. The field covers many varied and highly controversial topics, ranging from war journalism to Benetton advertising.

Media Ethics

Issues of moral principles and values as applied to the conduct, roles and content of the mass media in particular journalistic ethics and advertising ethics. In relation to news coverage it includes issues such as impartiality, objectivity, balance, bias, privacy and the public interest. More generally it also includes stereotyping, taste and decency, obscenity, freedom of speech, advertising practices such as product placement and legal issues such as defamation. On an institutional level it includes debates over media ownership and control commercialization, accountability the relation of the media to the political system, issues arising from regulation (e.g. censorship) and deregulation.

Ethics of Journalism

The ethics of journalism is one of the most well-defined branches of media ethics, primarily because it is frequently taught in schools of journalism. Journalistic ethics tends to dominate media ethics sometimes almost to the exclusion of other areas.

News Manipulation

News can manipulate and be manipulated. Governments and corporations may attempt to manipulate news media Governments. For example, by censorship, and corporations by share ownership. The methods of manipulation are subtle and many. Manipulation may be voluntary or involuntary Truth. Truth may conflict with many other values.

Public Interest

Revelation of military secrets and other sensitive government information may be contrary to the public interest, even if it is true. However, public interest is not a term which is easy to define. Media ethics are a complex topic because they deal with an institution that must do things that ordinary people in ordinary circumstances would not do. Media ethics draw on a range of philosophical principles, including basic Judeo-Christian values, Aristotle's ideas about virtue and balanced behaviors (the golden mean), Kant's categorical imperative, Mill's principle of utility, Rawls's veil of ignorance, and the Hutchins Commission's social-responsibility ethics. One way contemporary journalists can resolve their ethical problems is by using the Bok model for ethical decision making. Reporters face a range of ethical issues on a regular basis. Those issues include the following,

Truthfulness

Journalists need to make a commitment to telling the truth. This includes not giving false or made-up reports, and telling truthful stories that are not intended to deceive the audience. This may require reporters to provide not only the facts but also the context surrounding them. Truthfulness requires a commitment not only from the journalist but also from the organization he or she works for.

Conflicts of interest

The interests of a corporation that owns a news organization may sometimes be at odds with the nature of the news being reported. Journalists need to be careful not only to portray their parent company in an accurate light but also to give no special favors to companies connected to the organization's parent company.

Sensationalism

News organizations sometimes emphasize news that is interesting but unimportant. This happens when reporters put more effort into attracting and pleasing an audience than into reporting on the critical issues of the day. This can happen because of the increased pace of the news business brought about by cable television, the Internet, and the parent company's desire for profits.

Authenticity and appropriateness of photographs

Photos can be among the most controversial media materials, both because of their disturbing content and because they can be altered with digital editing tools.

Privacy

Salacious details of the lives of public figures is a central content element in many media. Publication is not necessarily justified simply because the information is true. Privacy is also a right, and one which conflicts with free speech. See: paparazzi.

Fantasy

Fantasy is an element of entertainment, which is a legitimate goal of media content.Journalism may mix fantasy and truth, with resulting ethical dilemmas.

See: National Enquirer, Jayson Blair scandal, Adnan Hajj photographs controversy.

Taste

Photo journalists who cover war and disasters confront situations which may shock the sensitivities of their audiences. For example, human remains are rarely screened. The ethical issue is how far should one risk shocking an audience's sensitivities in order to correctly and fully report the truth.

See photojournalism.

Conflict with the law

Journalistic ethics may conflict with the law over issues such as the protection of confidential news sources. There is also the question of the extent to which it is ethically acceptable to break the law in order to obtain news. For example, undercover reporters may be engaging in deception, trespass and similar torts and crimes. See undercover journalism, investigative journalism.

Ethics of Entertainment Media

Issues in the ethics of entertainment media include:

- The depiction of violence and sex, and the presence of strong language. Ethical guidelines and legislation in this area are common and many media (e.g. film, computer games) are subject to ratings systems and supervision by agencies. An extensive guide to international systems of enforcement can be found under motion picture rating system.

- Product placement. An increasingly common marketing tactic is the placement of products in entertainment media. The producers of such media may be paid high sums to display branded products. The practice is controversial and largely unregulated. Detailed article: product placement.

- Stereotypes. Both advertising and entertainment media make heavy use of stereotypes. Stereotypes may negatively affect people's perceptions of themselves or promote socially undesirable behavior. The stereotypical portrayals of men, affluence and ethnic groups are examples of major areas of debate.

- Taste and taboos. Entertainment media often questions of our values for artistic and entertainment purposes. Normative ethics is often about moral values, and what kinds should be enforced and protected. In media ethics, these two sides come into conflict. In the name of art, media may deliberately attempt to break with existing norms and shock the audience. That poses ethical problems when the norms abandoned are closely associated with certain relevant moral values or obligations. The extent to which this is acceptable is always a hotbed of ethical controversy.

Media and Democracy

In democratic countries, a special relationship exists between media and government. Although the freedom of the media may be constitutionally enshrined and have precise legal definition and enforcement, the exercise of that freedom by individual journalists is a matter of personal choice and ethics. Modern democratic government subsists in representation of millions by hundreds. For the representatives to be accountable and for the process of government to be transparent, effective communication paths must exist to their constituents. Today these paths consist primarily of the mass media to the extent that if press freedom disappeared, so would most political accountability. Media ethics merges with issues of civil rights and politics. Issues include:

- Subversion of media independence by financial interests.
- Government monitoring of media for intelligence gathering against its own people.

Media Integrity

Media integrity refers to the ability of a media outlet to serve the public interest and democratic process, making it resilient to institutional corruption within the media system,[3]economy of influence, conflicting dependence and political clientelism. Media integrity encompasses following qualities of a media outlet.

- Independence from private or political interests
- Transparency about own financial interests
- Commitment to journalism ethics and standards
- Responsiveness to citizens

Media Ethics and Media Economics

Media economics where things such as-deregulation of media, concentration of media ownership, FCC regulations in the U.S, media trade unions and labor issues and other such worldwide regulating bodies, citizen media (low power FM, community radio) have ethical implications.

Media Ethics and Public Officials

The media has manipulated the way public officials conduct themselves through the advancement of technology. Constant television coverage displays the legislative proceedings, exposing faster than ever before, unjust rulings throughout the government process. Truth telling is crucial in media ethics as any opposition of truth telling is considered deception. Anything shown by the media whether print or video is considered to be original. When a statement is written in an article or a video is shown of a public official, it is the original truthful words of the individual official themselves.

Similarities between Media Ethics and other Fields of Applied Ethics

Privacy and honesty are issues extensively covered in medical ethical literature, as is the principle of harm-avoidance. The trade-offs between economic goals and social values has been covered extensively in business ethics(as well as medical and environmental ethics).

Differences between Media Ethics and Other Fields of Applied Ethics

The issues of freedom of speech and aesthetic values (taste) are primarily at home in media ethics. However a number of further issues distinguish media ethics as a field in its own right. A theoretical issue peculiar to media ethics is the identity of observer and observed. The press is one of the primary guardians in a democratic society of many of the freedoms, rights and duties discussed by other fields of applied ethics. In media ethics the ethical obligations of the guardians themselves comes more strongly into the foreground.

A further self-preferentiality or circular characteristic in media ethics is the questioning of its own values. Meta-issues can become identical with the subject matter of media ethics. This is most strongly seen when artistic elements are considered.

Benetton advertisements and Turner prize candidates are both examples of ethically questionable media uses which question their own questioner.

Another characteristic of media ethics is the disparate nature of its goals. Ethical dilemmas emerge when goals conflict. The goals of media usage diverge sharply. Expressed in a consequentialist manner, media usage may be subject to pressures to maximize: economic profits, entertainment value, information provision, the upholding of democratic freedoms, the development of art and culture, fame and vanity.

Participants and Utilizes

A wide variety of people, such as teachers, military officers and non-commissioned officers, health care professionals, lawyers, accountants and engineers engage in professional development. Individuals may participate in professional development because of an interest in lifelong learning, a sense of moral obligation, to maintain and improve professional competence, to enhance career progression, to keep abreast of new technology and practices or to comply with professional regulatory requirements.

Approaches

In a broad sense, professional development may include formal types of vocational education, typically post-secondary or poly-technical training leading to qualification or credential required to obtain or retain employment. Professional development may also come in the form of pre-service or in-service professional development programs. These programs may be formal or informal, group or individualized. Individuals may pursue professional development independently or programs may be offered by human resource departments. Professional development on the job may develop or enhance process skills, sometimes referred to as leadership skills, as well as task skills. Some examples for process skills are 'effectiveness skills', 'team functioning skills', and 'systems thinking skills'.

Professional development opportunities can range from a single workshop to a semester-long academic course, to services offered by a medley of different professional development providers and varying widely with respect to the philosophy, content, and format of the learning experiences. Some examples of approaches to professional development include

- **Case Study Method**: The case method is a teaching approach that consists in presenting the students with a case, putting them in the role of a decision maker facing a problem.

- **Consultation**: To assist an individual or group of individuals to clarify and address immediate concerns by following a systematic problem-solving process.

- **Coaching**: To enhance a person's competencies in a specific skill area by providing a process of observation, reflection, and action.

- **Communities of Practice**: To improve professional practice by engaging in shared inquiry and learning with people who have a common goal

- **Lesson Study**: To solve practical dilemmas related to intervention or instruction through participation with other professionals in systematically examining practice

- **Mentoring**: To promote an individual's awareness and refinement of his or her own professional development by providing and recommending structured opportunities for reflection and observation

- **Reflective Supervision**: To support, develop, and ultimately evaluate the performance of employees through a process of inquiry that encourages their understanding and articulation of the rationale for their own practices

- **Technical Assistance**: To assist individuals and their organization to improve by offering resources and information, supporting networking and change efforts.

Initial

Initial professional development (IPD) is defined as a period of development during which an individual acquires a level of competence necessary in order to operate as an autonomous professional. Professional associations may recognize the successful completion of IPD by the award of chartered or similar status. Examples of IPD are the Institute of Mathematics and its Applications, the Institution of Structural Engineers and the Institution of Occupational Safety and Health.

Continuing

Continuing professional development(CPD) or continuing professional education(CPE) is continuing education to maintain knowledge and skills. Most professions have CPD obligations. Examples are the Royal Institution of Chartered Surveyors, American Academy of Financial Management, safety professionals with the International Institute of Risk&Safety Management (IIRSM) or the Institution of Occupational Safety and Health (IOSH),[22] and medical and legal professionals, who are subject to continuing medical education or continuing legal education requirements, which vary by jurisdiction.

Ethics of Professional Development

Professional ethics for the teaching profession are one profession of teachers and leaders in early childhood education and in primary and secondary schools. Our political mandate is to promote learning, development and building for all children and pupils. Our values, attitudes and actions influence the impact of our work. These ethical principles constitute a common ground for the development of our ethical awareness. It is our responsibility to act in accordance with these values and principles.

Basic Values of the Teaching Profession

Human Values and Human Rights

These rights must be promoted and defended in early childhood education and in schools. The inviolability of human individual freedom and the need for safety and care are fundamental.

Respect and Equality

Each individual person's personality and integrity must be met with respect. No form of oppression, indoctrination or prejudiced opinions shall be tolerated. All children in early childhood education and all pupils in schools have a right to participate and have their views heard and taken into account.

Professional Integrity

Ethical consciousness and high professional competence are the basis of the profession's integrity and are essential in creating good conditions for play, learning and building. Our right to methodological freedom and our professional discretion gives us a special responsibility to be open about our academic and pedagogical choices. Society should be confident that we use our professional autonomy both properly and ethically.

Privacy

Adherence to confidentiality and information standards is crucial in our work. Everyone has a right to privacy. Personal information must be managed in ways that protect the integrity and dignity of children, pupils, parents and colleagues. Teachers and leaders in education are committed to the professional ethics and can never shirk their professional responsibilities.

Chapter V

Inculcated Values

Education is a systematic attempt towards human learning. All learning is subjective and self-related. Educational activity starts with the individual. Education that is value-based. Education that imparts roots and also gives wings. The fact that all good education is, in essence a process of developing the human personality in all its dimensions-intellectual, physical, social ethical and moral is undisputed and universally accepted. Good education is inconceivable if it fails to inculcate values essential to good life and social wellbeing. Value orientation is integral to all stages of upbringing, formal education, interaction between individuals and social groups.

Values are inseparable from life of the individual. Since education is an essential requirement, an integral point of education, the aims of education, content and methodology is viewed in terms of value development. Human development cannot be conceived in the absence of values. The aim of education is growth or development both intellectual and moral. Education from the value development point of view is a scientific process of developing a desirable form of thinking and ability to deal with issues related to values. Values form a significant aspect of all the areas of development.

The phrase `Value Education' as used in the area of school education refers to the study of development of essential values in pupils and the practices suggested for the promotion of the same. Value education is education in values and education towards the inculcation of values. In its full range of meaning, value education includes developing the appropriate sensibilities moral, cultural, spiritual. Value education is essentially `Man Making' and `Character Building'.

Moral development is the axis on that revolves ones personality and character. Based on its nature, moral development has been studied as part of cognitive development, social learning and psychoanalytic dimensions. The outcome of the studies conducted by several development psychologists are very useful is deciding about the activities in value education for school children.

The recent term 'value education' is preferred to the traditional approaches such as moral education, religious education, social and character education, moral and spiritual education.

Moral or value education is to be effectively undertaken, it must be firmly based on the principles of value development. One of the distinguishing features of Indian philosophy is that throughout its long history, it has continuously given the foremost place to values. Our aims of value development and education are derived from this root. The content of communication media serves as the sources of values. Teachers and parents act as models for children to cultivate socially desirable behavioral patterns.

The pupils' learning of values in the school is a continuation of their learning in their family, community and through mass media. Therefore, the school should take into cognizance and utilize all types of social and educational influences affecting the development of values in pupils for value education purpose.

The children in the schools and colleges should be told about the religious concepts such as sin, virtue, faith and duty. The youth should be apprised of their duties in order to inspire them to contribute to the building of a modern and vibrant nation.

The methods and strategies of value education are many and varied the selection of that depends much upon the values chosen, sources of development of these values and many other limiting factors. The entire school curriculum function is an important source of value education. Values education in schools, therefore, is effected through direct, indirect, incidental methods. Values get transmitted via both the implicit or hidden and planned curriculum. The entire process of value education is a highly comprehensive and complex one that involves a wide range and variety of learning experiences.

Meaning

Through all curricular programmes, the following are important for inculcation of values by suitably introducing the element of values in every step:

1. **Knowing**: The learner must be made aware of the inherent values or ethical issues while going through a particular topic.
2. **Making Judgments**: The learner must be provided with conflicting situations while teaching/ learning to enable him/ her to evaluate the implications of the related values.
3. **Believing**: Emphasis should be given to relevant points helpful in development of faith in these related values.
4. **Action**: The learner may be encouraged to practice these values in actual life situations as a result of change in his/her behaviour brought about by relevant and meaningful experiences.

   Values are defined as everything from eternal ideas and guiding principles that lead to desirable behavioral patterns and are positive. They involve both the cognitive and affective dimensions and provide an important basis for individual choices based on connecting thoughts and feelings and emotions leading to positive action. Attitudes–are individual responses to other people or situations or even events that are shaped by their personal values. While positive human values-compassion, and caring, respect and tolerance for others are desirable they will find reflection in the attitude of nurturing, or destroying the environment, being kind or cruel towards animals, etc.

5. **Internalization:** A values centered approach in the classroom will add meaning to each class. Moreover as students engage creatively in the classroom, lesson objectives will be realized effectively. Anything that helps us to behave appropriately towards others adds to values of respect and courtesy. Anything that takes us out of ourselves, and inspires us to sacrifice for the good of others or for a great cause is of spiritual value.

Approaches

Value Inculcation, Analysis and Clarification

Values are those characteristics of human society that set norms, exert control and influence the thinking, willing, feeling and actions of individuals. The inculcation of values has been cherished as a noble goal of all societies of all times and India has been no exception to this. In India values are a national concern. The constitution of India lays the firm foundation of a sovereign, socialist, secular and democratic republic. It secures for all citizens social, economic and political justice, liberty of thought, expression, faith, belief and worship, equality of status and of opportunity, fraternity, assuming the dignity of the individual, and the unity and integrity of the nation. All these provisions along with the supremacy of the judiciary are the cornerstones of peace and harmony.

The Value Inculcation Approach

The value inculcation approach is an approach that lays emphasis on the inculcation of social values in students. This approach is actually a traditional approach. This approach is geared towards instilling and internalizing norms into person's own, value systems. This approach would help in molding the character of students to become good citizens, being as an imparted knowledge for their intellectual advancement. The process of acquiring values begins at birth. Values develop through life and evolve from life experiences. They are formed by combining: intellect, will, emotions and spiritual needs. A value is a guide, a norm, a principle by that a person lives. Values have seven criteria. These are as follows

- A value must be chosen freely.
- A value must be chosen from alternatives.
- A value must be chosen after considering the consequences.
- A value must be performed.
- A value becomes a pattern of life.
- A value is cherished.
- A value is publicly affirmed.

Value inculcation is building of the values in our inner core. This is a process that happens unconsciously but it is conscious as starting learning about values in school. Schools use three chief methods in moral education. These methods are:

- Inculcation
- Value clarification, and
- Value analysis

Inculcation is an effort to teach children the values that educators believe lead to moral behaviour. These values include honesty, compassion, justice, and respect for others. Through value inculcation approach may be forced to act on students according to specific desired values. A positive and negative reinforcement by the teacher helps value inculcation. The value inculcation is by no means a simple matter. There is no magic formula, technique or strategy for this. Value inculcation can be achieved' directly, indirectly or incidentally. Direct value inculcation refers to deliberate, systematic instruction given during the time of formation. Indirectly, value inculcation can be imparted through the regular subjects of the curriculum and co-curricular activities. Incidentally, value inculcation can be given through events and incidents related to good values occurring around us thus relating value inculcation to concrete situations. There are two important approaches in any inculcation of values. One approach is to transmit a preexisting set 'of values to others. This can take up various forms such as:

- The model form (models influence thoughts and actions.)
- The reward and punishment form
- The explanatory form identifying certain values and providing explanation for them
- The nagging form the manipulative form
- The transmittal liberal arts form

Science is generally considered as a repository of human 'values fostering among other things commitment to truth, independence in observation and thought, free inquiry, and free thought. The laws of science hold true everywhere in the world. The content and processes of science are inseparably linked with value inculcation and value nurturing. The need to produce students of science with responsibility are capable of grappling with the complexities of social issues. An effort should be made to plan curricula, write textbooks, organize co-curricular activities, and plan projects, so that science is delivered as a package helping one to develop values. Science teaching should be comprehensive. While inculcating values in the context of science, it should be taken care to use science as a deliberate instrument or vehicle for promoting values. As teachers could be involved in value inculcation through science should possess the following traits

- Be able to identify values underlying the content they teach.
- Act as role models by internalizing values and help students also internalize the same.
- Be able to analyze the needs of children, cultivate interest in science, motivate them and encourage them in the art of self-learning by becoming a partner in the process.
- Have an understanding of the art and science of developing human personality in all its aspects with emphasis on integration, harmony, truth, beauty and excellence.
- Acquire familiarity with new techniques of transacting the changing curriculum and appreciate the educational implications in the teaching—learning strategies.
- Have a cheerful disposition.
- Be willing to establish a close rapport with parents, community and NGOs Working on a voluntary basis to promote values.

The Value-Clarification Approach

Value clarification is a complex system of behavioral modification involving various concepts, ideas, and applications. In the current school systems, the level of intellectual ability has decreased to the point, many high school graduates are incapable of reading, writing and performing arithmetic at any mediocre level of competence. The public schools, through mandated curricula and teaching methodology, have minimized the importance of the development of mental-thinking-cognitive skills and instead have placed greater attention on the alteration of beliefs, values and behaviors. Value clarification helps students develop their own values and moral standards by teaching them a decision-making process. The learning procedures stress setting goals, choosing thoughtfully from alternatives, and acting on one's own convictions. It helps students to use both rational thinking and emotional awareness to examine personal behavior patterns and classify and actualize values.

Value Clarification is a technique for encouraging students to relate their thoughts and their feelings and thus enrich their awareness of their own values. The teacher will carefully prepare value-related exercises and discussion questions, giving the students clear instructions. These exercises and discussion questions provide students the opportunity to explore their values and beliefs in a safe environment, while giving structure to the discussion. Through exercises and discussion, students should be made aware of the influences to their values, and to explore and acknowledge what they truly value in their lives. As values are the driving force behind most of your decisions and actions, the class activities should focus on engaging students in exercises that force them to wrestle with their values as they apply to subjects such as war, family, future, and a whole range of human relationships and situations. The teacher will act as a mediator for class discussions, making sure that no student's values are disrespected or differing-opinions are put down.

Modeling is an approach in transmitting values. The value-clarification approach tries to help young people answer some of these questions and build their own value system. It is not a new approach. There have always been parents, teachers, and other educators who have sought ways to help young people think through values issues for themselves. This approach is based upon the principle of values relativity and that we should strive to clarify those values that are personally meaningful, that is, the values that make us more purposeful, productive and socially aware, and better critical thinkers.

Prizing and Cherishing

Students must become aware of the beliefs and behaviors they prize. Children learn to establish values through exercises in that they rank or compare items or opinions based on person.al preference. Once students are comfortable sharing their personal position, a barrage of moral dilemmas may be hurled at them.

Publicly Affirming

Students are compelled to state their positions, either in class discussions, in written exercises, or in personal journals.

Unfinished sentences and personal questions are popular value clarification strategies that help the student reveal and explore some of his attitudes, beliefs, actions, convictions, interests, aspirations, likes, dislikes, goals and purposes. It is important to remember that value clarification encourages students to choose their behavior based in part on their feelings. The way a child feels about something is more important than actual realities.

Teachers can cultivate mutual respect among students while avoiding confrontations in class by promoting non- judgmental, empathetic, effective listening skills. Conditioned to remain calm, kind, and accepting no matter that comes up in class, students patiently hear out opposing viewpoints. Youth are discouraged from stating their convictions or from leaving a conversation should it prove to be an occasion of sin or offensive to modesty. Rather, students should suspend their own value judgments so as to understand the speaker's thoughts and feelings as he himself experiences them. Students then consider the new information in light of their existing beliefs, and decide if their values should be adjusted.

Children are not warned but some people can hurt them or lead them to sin. In reality these lessons encourage children to interact with pedophiles, drug pushers, and gang members, just as they would with virtuous people.

Acting

Students are prompted to demonstrate their beliefs. Within the confines of school activities, this may be as simple as writing a letter to the mayor, participating in a food drive for the poor, or planting trees in a city park. Students may be encouraged to take part in some movement to change society.

Acting with a Pattern, Consistency and Repetition

Students are taught that their behavior and choices should consistently reflect their values. If a particular student were to find it difficult or unconscionable to repeat an act, then the student would be encouraged to re-evaluate the value in terms of benefits and consequences vas pertinent to his personal circumstances and goals and to adjust his behavior accordingly in pursuit of self-fulfillment.

Students learn to weigh the pros and cons, the consequences of the various alternatives. The teacher also helps the students to consider whether their actions match their stated beliefs and if not, bring the two into closer harmony.

Value Analysis

The approach emphasizes rational thinking and reasoning. The purpose of the analysis approach is to help students to use logical thinking and the procedures of scientific investigation in dealing with value issues. Students are urged to provide verifiable facts about the correctness or value of the topics or issues under investigation. A major assumption is that valuing the cognitive process of determining and justifying facts and beliefs derived from those facts. The rationalist and empiricist views of human nature seem to provide the philosophical basis for this approach. The teaching methods used by this approach generally center around individual and group study of social value problems and issues, library and field research, and rational class discussions. These are techniques widely used in social studies instruction.

A variety of higher-order cognitive and intellectual operations are frequently used. They should be able to deal rationally with questions. There are a number of value analysis approaches available and all represent a systematic and structured way to attack an ethical problem. The value analysis movement is really taking the subject matter that is part of university level education and revising it so that it is suitable to be taught to high school and elementary students.

These include:

- Stating the issues
- Questioning and substantiating in the relevance of statements
- Applying analogous cases to qualify and refine value positions
- Pointing out logical and empirical inconsistencies in arguments
- Weighing counter arguments and
- Seeking and testing evidence.

A representative instructional model is presented by Metcalf (1971) are as follows:

- Identify and clarity the value question
- Assemble purported facts
- Assess the truth of purported facts
- Clarify the relevance of facts
- Arrive at a tentative value decision and
- Test the value principle implied in the decision.

Generally, this approach helps to develop reasoning powers, value judgments and value clarification skills and enhances thinking, speaking, and reasoning powers. It is an interesting means of providing training to students to deal with social issues in a rational manner and also to deal with value conflicts effectively.

Teaching Strategies

Curricular and Co-curricular Programmes

Human values are taught as well as caught. Value education is an integral part of the school system. A separate subject as value education is yet not acceptable to many educationists. A teacher has to identify chapters, topics and concepts from the subject through and can inculcate values. Almost all commissions and committees on value education recommended both curricular and co-curricular strategies to inculcation of values. The goal of providing value education is to develop in children, awareness, sensitivity, appreciation, reflective thinking about social/moral ethical values, provide them opportunity to make judgments of the right decisions. The traditional approach in imparting education focuses on providing knowledge and information to students as symbolized in the syllabus, that they are expected to memorize. They receive information but not education. The centre of attention is the subject matter. The instructional goal of education must be making students to understand, appreciate and learn the values inherent in the subject.

Value-based Curricular: Activities

The idea of providing vague education through the school subjects should not mean that the school subjects are to be treated mere vehicles of value education and not the knowledge of the discipline. Inculcating values with teaching of subjects is aimed at building holistic attitudes, positive feelings and emotions about the subject content during teaching-learning process and thereby guiding and facilitating acceptance and internalization of values. The teaching of different school subjects, therefore, should stir the processes involved in value development not only at knowing but also at the feeling and doing levels. The strategies that are applicable in regard to imparting knowledge and information may not be applicable in regard to education for values.

Curriculum with both the explicit and hidden, serves as an important source of value education. Curriculum seeks to transmit values through school subjects, the textbooks and transaction of the subject matter.

Value-based Co-curricular Activities

The co-curricular approach emphasizes the values through physical education, (sports, etc.), music education, art, family living, health, cultural program, festival celebration and any of the other augmentative curriculum areas. Teachers would be encouraged to use combinatorial sets of strategies to make every lesson, more meaningful, effective and in motivating the students. For-this purpose the suggested strategies would include problem solving (i) discussion (ii) project work (iii) storytelling (iv) acting (v) singing (vi) simulation games, Imparting knowledge, imbibing values for shaping their behaviors, the most effective teaching strategies would be (i) storytelling (ii) acting (iii) singing.

Value Inculcation through Personal Examples of Great and Noble Persons

Personal examples help students to deepen understanding, motivation, and responsibility with regard to making personal and social choices and to inspire individuals to choose their own personal, social, moral, and spiritual values and be aware of practical methods for developing and deepening them. Autobiographies, biographies and experiences of great and noble persons also provide inspiring values to the learners. Abdul Kalam's advice to young generation to, 'Dream always' may inspire children to be dreamers as well as doers to realize their dreams. Our youngsters can learn from the life experiences of these great and noble people that they achieved heights of greatness through sheer hard work, devotion, perseverance and determination. Lives of all great men remind us that we can also make our lives sublime. Abrham Lincon's letter to the teacher of his son may make a person learn value of self-respect.

Value Inculcation through different Characters

A teacher is an immediate and most important role model and must use recitation, storytelling, role play and dramatization to instill these values in the students. They can also use techniques of discussion, questioning and analysis and brainstorming to inculcate these values. A good teacher can go even beyond classroom and include community to instill fine values through practical examples, and demonstrations.

Inculcating the value of unity

Learning from Nature

Teacher can tell or read stories about animals that demonstrate unity, such as dolphins and elephants. There are many stories about dolphins saving humans. Teachers can tell many other stories about animal behaviour that demonstrates unity and cooperation. While doing this storytelling activities, students may be divided into several, groups. Teacher may ask each group .to study an animal known for support of its kind and discuss the following reflection points in regard to the animal studied. Unity creates a sense of belonging and increases well-being for all. The greatness of unity is that everyone is respected

Dramatization

"The future of our nation depends on our ability to create and to be creative. During the coming decades our most important national resources will be human resources. If our nation is to continue to meet the challenges of the future, todays schools need to develop creative leaders. Nowadays dramatic arts are .an important means of stimulating creativity in problem solving.

The Necessity for Institutional Moral Code

An institution could decide its moral code to practice the following principles such as

- Minimize the harm cause.
- Maximize the good cause.
- Be fair to all concerned.
- Have concern for being truthful.
- Respect the autonomy of others when they are pursuing legitimate actions etc.

Twenty first century needs to pay more attention to many aspects of caring including

- Caring for oneself, including one's health
- Caring for one's family friends and peers
- Caring for other people
- Caring for the social, economic, and ecological welfare of one's society and nation
- Caring for human rights
- Caring for the livability of the earth and
- Caring for truth, knowledge and learning

The Recommendations of NPE (1986) are

Encourage children to make choices and make them freely.

- Help them discover and examine available alternatives when faced with choices
- Help children weigh alternatives thoughtfully. Reflecting on the consequences of each
- Encourage children to consider what it is they, prize and cherish
- Give them opportunities to make public affirmation of their choices
- Encourage them to act, behave, live in accordance with their choices and
- Help them to examine repeated behaviors on patterns in their life.

Reward and Punishment Approach

Another dimension of value education is to avoid developing obnoxious habits and make them to achieve desirable behaviour. Time moves slowly to them and therefore, instead of being told the ultimate gain in the practice of a value, children should be given immediate reward on their success of a desirable behaviour.

Recommendations of Committees and Commissions Regarding value Education

In the 20 Century, several committees and three commissions on education in India were formed and they gave a number of suggestions to improve and strengthen Indian education. Many of them gave suggestions also in favour of Value education. A publication of the NCERT entitled 'A Symphony of Value education' (2001) is a compilation of the core suggestions in regard to Value education of all of them for the purpose of teacher educators and the B.Ed. students.

Report of Zakir Husain Committee (Basic National Education) (1938)

1. Report of the Religious Education Committee of the CABE (1846)
2. Report of the University Education Commission (Radhakrishnan Commission) (1948-49)
3. Report of the Secondary Education Commission (Mudaliar Commission) (1952-53).
4. Report of the Committee on Religious and Moral Instruction (Sri Praknsh Committee) (1960)
5. Report of the Education Commission (Kothari Commission) (1964- 66)
6. Report of the Committee of MPs on National Policy on Education (1967)
7. Report of the High Level Seminar on Value Oriented Education Organized by the NCERT at Shimla (1991)
8. Report of the National Policy on Education (1968)
9. Report of the Working Group to Review Teachers' Training Programme (1983)
10. Report of the National Policy on Education (1986)
11. Report of the Committee for Review of National Policy on Education 1986 (1990)
12. Report of the Core Group on Value Orientation of Education, GOT (1992)

Need for Value Education in 21st Century

The 21st century promises to be a time of scientific and technological growth at a level never before experienced in human history. This growth will either trigger chaos, disruption, war, starvation and disease or will introduce a period of humanistic cooperation, development, progress, and peace. The value choices that must be deliberately chosen and not left to chance must be secular, global, democratic, and pluralistic.

The Indian education system has changed from Gurukulum education to cyberspace education. The last two decades have witnessed a paradigm shift in the process of imparting and learning education. The values and ethics, that promote qualities makes an individual socially effective and happy, inculcate friendliness, co-cooperativeness, compassionate, self-disciplined, tolerant fearless, honest, truthful, dependable, courteous and having love for social justice. The growing concern over the erosion of essential values and pervasive cynicism has brought to focus the need for readjustments in the curriculum in order to make education a forceful tool for the cultivation of social and moral values.

Values are desirable and important, they are held in high esteem by any society in a person lives. Young people of the 21st century look for people who can be role models and guides. Lifestyle of young people is influenced by peer groups because of sociological reasons. Today there are new challenges, new dreams, new expectations and new questions propelled by latent doubts amidst those, should guide correctly channelizing their potentials and talents in meaningful routes. It is found that there is erosion in long accepted values and ethics is caught between increasing stress and strain. Social environments cause prejudices and complexes, hindering promotion of equality coupled with increasingly polluted and depleted natural resources, youngsters face a great threat to the quality of life.

The demands of the following three objectives to be fulfilled.

- To protect and enhance or natural unity.
- To preserve and defend or natural sovereignty
- To advance the cause of social justice.

Value education should provide possible solutions to challenges and opportunities presented by the complex, dynamic and global world. There is no magic formula, technique or strategy for this. Value education being a need of the hour is 21st century involves developing sensitivity to values, an ability to choose the right values in accordance with one's concept of the higher ideals of the life and internalizing them, realizing them in one's life and living in accordance with them. Therefore it is a lifelong quest and must be inculcated by the influence of a complex network of environmental factors such as home, parents, peer group, country, media and society at large. The three human functions head for knowledge, heart for feeling, and hand for action should play a role. Knowledge, idea and concepts that are accepted and acknowledged must be with conviction and commitment blooming fully for excellence in the three domains such as cognitive, affective and psychomotor. To achieve and make real, this concept of a world of peace for the 21st century the following humanistic values provide the basic essentials.

References

Aruna Goel & S L Goel (2005). *Human Values and Education*. New Delhi: Deep and Deep

Bharnderi, R.S (2003). *Value Education*. Chandigarh: Abishek Publications.

Charaborty, Mohit (1997). *Value Education: Changing Perspectives*. New Delhi: Krishna Publishers

Dhananjay Joshi (2006). *Value Education in Global Perspective*. New Delhi: Lotus Press.

Ghose, D.N (2005). *A Text Book of Value Education*. New Delhi: Dominant Publishers

Ignachimuthu, S (2008). *Values for Life*. Mumbai: Better You Books.

Kelly,G (1995). *The Psychology of Personal Constructs*. New York: W.W.Norton.

Kirshenbaum, H. (1983). *Advanced Values Clarifications*. California: University Associate Publications

Kirubha Charles & Arul Selvi, V (2012). *Peace and Value Education*. Hyderabad: Neelkamal

Kirubha Charles & Arul Selvi, V (2012). *Value Education*. New Delhi: Neelkamal

Kohlberg, L(1976). *Moral Development and Behaviour. Moral Stages and Moralizations*. CBS College Publishing: Holt and Winston.

Passi, B.K and Prabhakar Signh (2005). *Value Education*. Agra: National Psychological Corporations.

Raths, L.S and Simon, S.B (1978). *Values and Teaching*. Columbus: Ohio.

Ruhela, S.P & Rajkumar Nayak (2011). *Value education and Human Rights education*. New Delhi: Neelkamal

Saikia, Mukul (2012) *Higher Education and Inculcation of Values in Higher Education*. Bhiwani: Lakshmi Books

Simon, S., Howe, L., & Kirschenbaum, H. (1972). *Values clarification: A handbook of practical strategies for teachers and students*. New York: Social Science Education Consortium.

Subrahmanyam, K (1994). *Education in Values*. Madeas: Vivekananda Kendra Prakasham.

Venkataiah, N (2005). *Value Education*. New Delhi: APH Publications